VICTORY ON ICE

The Chicago Blackhawks'

First Stanley Cups

PAUL R. GREENLAND

NORTH HILL BOOKS

Every effort has been made to trace the ownership of copyrighted photographs that appear in this book. The author would appreciate notification of any errors or omissions and will gladly make changes in future printings.

ISBNs: 978-0-9659128-1-5

North Hill Books
5062 Rockrose Ct., Suite 209
Roscoe, IL 60173
info@nhillbooks.com

Front cover illustration by Holly Tempka
Back cover photos: Autographed stick and ticket stub images courtesy of the Art Wiebe family. Stanley Cup photo courtesy of Ty Dilello/Manitoba Hockey Hall of Fame.
Book design and typesetting by Mayfly Design

Publisher's Cataloging-in-Publication Data
Names: Greenland, Paul R., 1971- author.
Title: Victory on ice : the Chicago Blackhawks' first Stanley Cups / Paul R. Greenland.
Other titles: Chicago Blackhawks' first Stanley Cups.
Description: First printing. | Roscoe, IL : North Hill Books, [2023] | Includes
    bibliographical references.
Identifiers: ISBN: 978-0-9659128-1-5 (paperback) | LCCN: 2022919156
Subjects: LCSH: Chicago Blackhawks (Hockey team)—History. | Hockey players—
    Illinois—Chicago—History—20th century. | Stanley Cup (Hockey) (1934) | Stanley
    Cup (Hockey) (1938) | Hockey—Illinois—Chicago—History. | National Hockey
    League—History. | Chicago (Ill.)— History—20th century. | Depressions—1929—
    Illinois—Chicago. | BISAC: SPORTS & RECREATION / Winter Sports / Hockey. |
    HISTORY / United States / State & Local / Midwest.
Classification: LCC: GV848.C48 G74 2023 | DDC: 796.962/640977311—dc23

Library of Congress Control Number: 2022919156
First Printing: 2022
Printed in the United States of America

To my father, Rollin Greenland.

James, Rollin, and Richard Greenland (left to right) pose on their homemade car in September 1941, shortly after the Great Depression and about three months before the United States entered World War II.

In memory of my aunt, Anna Marie (Carlson) Isabelli (1928–2022)

Anna Marie Carlson at the World's Fair in Chicago on September 1, 1934.

Contents

SECTION I: HOCKEY, CHICAGO, AND THE GREAT DEPRESSION

SECTION II: 1933–34 STANLEY CUP

SECTION III: 1937–38 STANLEY CUP

Acknowledgments

The author would like to thank the following individuals and organizations, without whom this book would not have been possible:

- Bethany G. Anderson, University Archives, University of Illinois at Urbana-Champaign
- Julia Bachrach, Chicago Park District
- George Bathje
- Katie Blank, Marquette University, Special Collections & University Archives
- Boston Public Library
- Elizabeth Buzenius
- Marya Callahan
- Craig Campbell, D.K. (Doc) Seaman Hockey Resource Centre, Hockey Hall of Fame
- Chicago History Museum
- Rachel Cole, Transportation Library, Northwestern University Libraries
- Bob Cullum and the Family of Leslie R. Jones
- Barbara Davidson
- Ty Dilello
- Gail Dupar
- Scott Fisher
- Bill Fitsell
- Kevin Friesen
- Pam Poulter Friesen
- Roger Godin

- Adam Gottselig
- Greg Gottselig
- Mark Hemstock
- Hockey Hall of Fame
- Dale Hornickel
- Ruth Dahlstrom Jewett
- Virgil C. Johnson
- Ross Judge, HockeyGods.com
- Joan Karakas
- Barbara Lanphier, Illinois Railway Museum, Strahorn Library
- Kevin B. Leonard, Northwestern University Archives
- Manitoba Hockey Hall of Fame
- Jean McKean
- Castle McLaughlin
- Jeff Miclash
- Bruce Moffat, Chicago Transit Authority
- Jay Pederson
- Edna Poulter
- Virginia (Romnes) Hansen
- Julie Scheife, Mayfly Design
- Ryan Scheife, Mayfly Design
- Society for International Hockey Research
- Kenneth Spengler, Illinois Railway Museum, Strahorn Library
- William Sproule
- Laurie Stein, History Center of Lake Forest-Lake Bluff
- Morag Walsh, Special Collections, Chicago Public Library

Foreword

When it opened in 1929, the Chicago Stadium was the country's largest indoor auditorium and housed colossal events that elevated people from the grim realities of long breadlines, brothers sparing dimes, and, later, of wartime's uncertainty and devastation. While Chicago's motto, *I WILL*, is a testament to civic gumption and perseverance, *TO WIN* could be safely said to be the motto of the city's premier hockey team, the beloved Black Hawks. The team proudly called the handsome edifice on West Madison Street home until 1994, when it was torn down. Meeting the aspirations of the public is a principal role of a sports team, and, in an abstract sense, winning on the ice kept the crowd's positive attention on the larger intangible worldwide issues around them. Above all, *TO WIN*.

Virgil Johnson, my Minneapolis-born father, was scouted in 1937 and became a member of the Black Hawks "Cinderella" 1937–38 team. He joined the Hawks sometime in mid-season, reenforcing owner Frederic McLaughlin's desire to have an American players team. American players for an American audience. Whether this noble goal was by necessity or just ambitious manipulation we do not know. But the gamble paid off. Four Minnesota players, Doc Romnes, Mike Karakas, Cully Dahlstrom, and my father, all longtime friends, were signed up between 1932 and 1937. That somewhat leveled the numerical balance between Canadian and American teammates with the Black Hawks. Salaries for the players in those early days were higher than the median salary that a middle-class family earned (about $2,000). They were paid premiums in tournament finals on a per-game basis. The pressure was to win so that you could remain.

The team and families lived together in Chicago's historic Hotel Guyon. The players had hockey practice by day and games by night. While the men skated to glory, their wives volunteered in soup kitchens and sewing/knitting circles. My mother could knit a pair of children's mittens during a game. During World War II, she was selling War Bonds on State Street and dancing with young servicemen in the canteen before they were shipped overseas. She wrote to many of them abroad biweekly during the war. We children were "wrangled" by a gal who marched us over to the Conservatory in Garfield Park. That is when we weren't riding up and down in the elevators ogling the swell lady elevator operators. A real treat was to be taken to Lincoln Park Zoo. Living conditions in the Hotel Guyon were far from the luxury one sees with the hockey stars' families today. It was like a dormitory. The Johnson residence was one room with a kitchenette. We later added a bedroom when one became available for a dollar more rent. A trundle bed would go up and down in the living room creating more space by day. It was heaven!

As anyone who has an athlete for a parent knows, all activities rotate around the "star." When to get up, when to go to bed. In public events, we stood respectfully behind him. Mother rehearsed me as a small person to shake hands with a squeeze, not to offer a "limp rag," to look up at an adult in the eye and ask them something about themselves and not chatter away about myself. Food was always heavy on the protein. My father could eat a steak every night of the week, always with baked potatoes. These were the rationing and Depression-era years, but the fans compensated by pressing food stamps into my parents' hands to keep the team fed. And there was drinking. Yes, beer was a staple, but some players were all too friendly with John Barleycorn.

My father finally skated off the ice in 1952 after more than two decades in professional hockey. His glory years were 1930 to 1945, when he retired from the Black Hawks. Despite the Great Depression and World War II as the backdrop for his career, he was never out of work. He was not drafted into the military, became a family man, played hockey during the season and worked in carpentry and even mowed lawns in Lakewood Cemetery back home in the summers. "I never got rich, when we won the Stanley Cup in '38," my father remembered. "We got $500 and a watch."

This period has faded from our national memory. And it was only 80 years ago. No period in history exists without something that has gone before and events that come after. McLaughlin set the stage for the emerging "star" American Player, but winning is transitory. The Black Hawks only won the Stanley Cup three times in the 20th century, and two of those years were in the 1930s. Paul Greenland has done some fine excavation here to bring that early story back to Center Ice, and I commend him for his expertise and tireless effort. Hockey remains a great sport. A fast sport that requires considerable skill. Its managers and players, then and now, deserve our attention and applause.

—Virgil C. Johnson, June 29, 2022

Introduction

The inspiration for this book dates back to January 27, 1992, when I placed a long-distance call to Sun City, Arizona. After a few rings, I heard a voice that had been echoing through Chicago Blackhawks history since 1928, when Harold "Mush" March became one of the team's earliest players. When his puck-shooting days were over in 1945, after 759 games, Mush stayed on the ice for another nine years as an NHL linesman. At 83, he was still golfing three to four times per week. I was barely 20, had never interviewed anyone, or written anything for publication. Mush probably did not realize that I was just a kid, and that in the world of writers and authors, I was as unknown and green as they came.

Back then, Ed Belfour, Chris Chelios, Jeremy Roenick, and Steve Larmer were my heroes. Pat Foley and Dale Tallon called games from the Madhouse on Madison. The previous summer, I had started researching what eventually became *Hockey Chicago Style*, an authorized history of the Blackhawks. Mush was the first of more than 40 players, coaches, and officials I interviewed for that project. But it was only fitting, because his name was synonymous with firsts. Mush scored the very first goal at Maple Leaf Gardens in 1931, and the goal that gave Chicago its first Stanley Cup in 1934.

When the final game was played at the Gardens in February 1999, Mush joined former Maple Leaf Red Horner, his one-time enemy, in a ceremonial puck drop, using the actual "first goal" puck from 1931. The year before he died, Mush dropped the puck for the 2000–01 season opener at United Center. Sadly, he was not there to see his old team win the Stanley Cup in 2010, 2013, and 2015. Following the third victory, NHL Commissioner Gary Bettman declared the Blackhawks a "dynasty." The proclamation sparked more than a few debates but was widely accepted. Dynasty or not, a new era of NHL hockey had arrived in Chicago, defined by modern-day heroes like Corey Crawford, Patrick Kane, and Jonathan Toews.

Chicago's recent Stanley Cup wins are fresh in the city's collective hockey psyche. The 1961 championship, which happened six decades ago, can still be recalled by well-seasoned fans. Thanks to rekindled relationships between the team and icons like Bobby Hull and the late Stan Mikita, these greats of yesteryear became a more visible part of the United Center landscape. Their last names still appear on the backs of fans' jerseys.

Most committed followers know the Blackhawks won Stanley Cups in 1934 and 1938, but these milestones, which happened a very long time ago—well before the "dynasty"—are seldom discussed and often overlooked. On April 14, 1994, the Blackhawks played their very last regular season game at Chicago Stadium. The cover of that night's 72-page souvenir game program carried the tagline, "Remember the Roar," in honor of the legendary arena. A full-page photo of the 1960–61 Stanley Cup team appears midway through the book, along with tributes to legends Tony Esposito, Glenn Hall, Bobby Hull, and Stan Mikita. An entire page is devoted to Al Secord, but photos of the 1933–34 and 1937–38 Stanley Cup teams are missing.

Their absence is unfortunate, because these early championship teams initiated the "roar" that fans were being encouraged to remember. Long before Tony "O" and Mr. Goalie made their marks as puck stoppers and the Golden Jet and Stosh became scoring legends, an earlier generation of players electrified Stadium crowds. Chicago's early hockey milestones were attained by players who were the superstars of their day. Many were pioneers, and some were enshrined in the Hockey Hall of Fame, the United States Hockey Hall of Fame, and numerous Canadian provincial halls of fame.

Like life itself, hockey was different during the Blackhawks' formative years. In a later interview, Mush recalled the early days of his career when hockey players earned meager salaries. "It was a different time," he said, remembering a game that was slower, but also tougher, with longer shifts for players, no helmets, modest protective equipment, brutal physical play, and locker rooms that were anything but plush.

Many players and their families lived in Chicago's Garfield Park neighborhood, in small apartments and hotels where they did life together, celebrating birthdays, cooking meals, playing games, and watching out for each other. Some took the bus to practices and games at the Stadium. Travel between Chicago and other NHL cities involved long train rides. Camaraderie was strengthened aboard Pullman cars, where players smoked cigarettes, played cards, and engaged in practical jokes.

When I described this project to other hockey authors and researchers, more than one said the Chicago Blackhawks' early history has never been honored very well. This did not surprise me, but it confirmed that my efforts were meaningful. So did the remembrances of the many families I connected with. Sons, daughters, nieces, nephews, and grandchildren of former players generously took the time to recall not just hockey accomplishments, but the kind of people their ancestors were. The photographs, scrapbook pages, telegrams, and letters they provided helped me to re-create scenes from Chicago's golden era of hockey, which is worth remembering and celebrating.

The quest for Chicago's first Stanley Cup unfolded against the backdrop of the World's Fair, an exciting event that inspired millions of people to experience the latest wonders, even as the Great Depression imposed incredible suffering and hardship on the nation. Victory was achieved with legendary players like offensive powerhouse Paul Thompson, who led the Blackhawks in scoring for six consecutive seasons; defensemen Lionel "Big Train" Conacher, who later became Canada's "Athlete of the Half Century" for his athletic prowess in multiple sports; and Chuck Gardiner, one of the greatest goaltenders in NHL history. Chicago's heart was broken when Gardiner died the summer after the 1934 victory, as did rookie forward Jack "Newsy" Leswick, whose body was recovered from a muddy Winnipeg river, less his gold Stanley Cup watch.

This book ends with coverage of the 1938 Stanley Cup finals—one of the greatest Cinderella stories in professional sports. After winning just 14 of 48 regular season games, the Blackhawks won the Stanley Cup under coach Bill Stewart. An NHL referee and Major League Baseball umpire by trade, Stewart was the first American to lead an NHL team to hockey's ultimate prize. In the nets that season was "Iron Mike" Karakas, the first American-born goalie to play in the NHL. Earl Seibert, the bone-crushing "Big Dutchman," patrolled Chicago's blue line, striking fear in the hearts of opponents, including Boston's notorious Eddie Shore.

By resurrecting, honoring, and preserving the Blackhawks' first two championships, I have attempted to fill a void in the canon of sports books. *Victory on Ice* recreates a near-century-old landscape, taking readers beyond scores and statistics and allowing them to grasp what it was like to be a professional hockey player in Chicago during the 1930s. It is a tribute to the generation that ignited the roar that echoes through United Center today.

—Paul R. Greenland, July 25, 2022

Author's Notes

The Chicago Black Hawks' name changed to Chicago Blackhawks in 1986. While the latter version of the name is mainly used throughout this book, readers will see the former version in the foreword and material that is quoted directly from earlier sources.

Two chapters profile players from the 1933–34 and 1937–38 Stanley Cup teams. They include boxes that contain athletes' names, birth and death dates (when known), key statistics, and other pertinent information. Uniform numbers, games played, goals, assists, points, penalty minutes, and seasons are specific only to the Chicago Blackhawks and were obtained directly from the team's media guide. Birthplaces, birth and death dates, and honors and awards (including All-Star team nominations, trophies, and halls of fame inductions, which pertain to a player's entire career, were obtained from a combination of sources, namely *Inside Sports Hockey* (formerly *The Complete Encyclopedia of Hockey*), *Total Hockey: The Official Encyclopedia of the National Hockey League*, the Hockey Hall of Fame, the United States Hockey Hall of Fame, and other provincial and national halls of fame, including:

- British Columbia Hockey Hall of Fame
- British Columbia Sports Hall of Fame
- Canada's Sports Hall of Fame
- International Hockey Hall of Fame
- Manitoba Hockey Hall of Fame
- Manitoba Sports Hall of Fame
- Ontario Sports Hall of Fame

- Saskatchewan Hockey Hall of Fame
- Saskatchewan Sports Hall of Fame

While conducting research for this book, the author encountered instances where highly reputable sources offered conflicting information. In most cases, this pertained to player facts and statistics, including name spellings, birth and death dates, and details regarding minor league teams. Every effort has been made to obtain accurate information, and the author regrets any errors.

Throughout the text, many junior, senior, minor, and professional hockey leagues are referenced, mainly in player biographies. In most cases, a league's name is spelled out entirely upon the first reference and abbreviated thereafter. For the reader's convenience, a list of these leagues appears here:

- All-American Hockey League (AAHL)
- American Hockey Association (AHA)
- American Hockey League (AHL)
- Canadian Professional Hockey League (Can-Pro)
- Canadian-American Hockey League (Can-Am)
- Central Hockey League (CHL)
- City and District Junior Hockey Leagues (City Jr.)
- City and District Senior Hockey Leagues (City Sr.)
- Eastern Hockey League (EHL)
- International-American Hockey League (IAHL)
- Manitoba Junior Hockey League (MJHL)
- Manitoba Senior Hockey League (MSHL)
- Montreal City Hockey League (MCHL)
- Ontario Hockey Association (OHA)
- Ontario Hockey Association Senior A (OHA Sr.)
- Ontario Hockey League (OHL)
- Prairie Hockey League (PrHL)
- Saskatchewan Junior Hockey League (SJHL)
- Saskatchewan Senior Hockey League (SSHL)
- Thunder Bay Senior Hockey League (TBSHL)
- Toronto and District Senior Hockey Leagues (Tor-Sr.)

- United States Hockey League (USHL)
- United States (Pro) Hockey League (USHL)
- United States Amateur Hockey Association (USAHA)
- Western Canada Hockey League (WCHL)

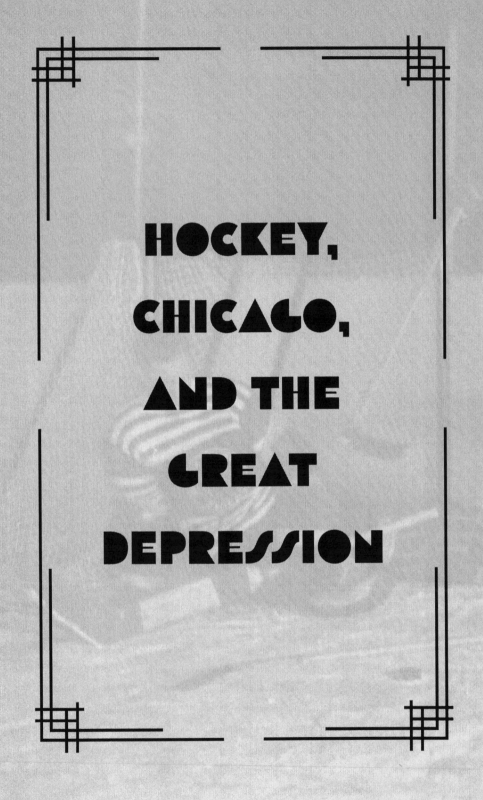

HOCKEY, CHICAGO, AND THE GREAT DEPRESSION

CHAPTER 1

Hard Knock Hockey

On a cold Sunday night in November, 14,500 hockey fans struggle to stay awake inside Chicago Stadium as an uneventful game between the Chicago Blackhawks and Toronto Maple Leafs crawls through a final minute of overtime. The score is tied at 1 and no goals have been scored since the first period. Although the Blackhawks are heroes for winning the city's first Stanley Cup two seasons before, the crowd probably wishes their tickets would have yielded more excitement. The Great Depression has a strong chokehold on almost everyone in 1936, and even the cheap seats are a sacrifice for most.

Just as the Stadium's clock is about to expire, Chicago forward Harold "Mush" March glides past the Toronto bench. In a flash, his fists connect with opponent Nick Metz. The fight is fair until the Maple Leafs' enforcer, Reginald "Red" Horner, leans over the boards and carves a gash over March's left eye with his stick, and another on his chin.

War has been declared before the first drop of Mush's blood splashes onto the ice. Led by scoring ace Paul Thompson, a swarm of Blackhawks rushes toward the Toronto bench. Thompson darts after Horner, a longtime personal enemy, disappearing into a wild mass of fighting players.

(opposite) Harold "Mush" March in 1933. (SDN-073825, Chicago Sun-Times/Chicago Daily News collection, Chicago History Museum)

The cavernous Chicago Stadium. (DN-0090385, Chicago Sun-Times/Chicago Daily News collection, Chicago History Museum)

Filled with vengeance, the once sleepy crowd erupts from the Stadium's red wooden seats. When Toronto's Harvey Jackson swings his stick at advancing spectators, the situation begins spiraling out of control. Chicago defenseman Earl Seibert quells a potential riot by reaching Jackson before the crowd does, delivering a blow that sends Jackson to the ice.

The Madhouse on Madison is without police protection tonight, thanks to a dispute between the Chicago Police Department and management over complimentary tickets. As the violence escalates, Andy Frain, head of the city's sports ushers, intervenes five minutes into the turmoil but is struck twice on the chin. Other ushers share his fate. One is clobbered by Chicago coach Clem Loughlin, who has no intention of being restrained.

The battle between players, ushers, and fans continues for another seven minutes. More slugging ensues between the original participants, including March and Metz, Thompson and Horner, and Seibert and Jackson. The fighting finally stops when Blackhawks owner Major Frederic McLaughlin walks onto the ice, joining referee Duke McCurry.

The smoke clears, revealing many bruised hands, black eyes, and bleeding wounds. Several players are taken to the hospital, including March and Toronto forward Frank "The Shawville Express" Finnigan, who needs stitches over his right eye, thanks to the handiwork of an enthusiastic spectator. The next morning, Chicago Police meet to discuss the need for law and order at the Stadium.

Although his presence had a calming effect, McLaughlin was likely thrilled about every punch his Blackhawks landed that night. The Major's patriotic fervor was stronger than ever in 1936–37. That season, he attempted to debut a team of only American-born players, angering many people in the hockey world, not to mention some of his own Canadian skaters.

Complex and perhaps misunderstood, the Major knew little about hockey when he became an NHL team owner in 1926. Yet, he possessed the right mix of drive, intensity, competitiveness, patriotism, wit, Irish temper, and intestinal fortitude to back an essentially unknown Canadian sport in the Midwest and lead it through the darkness and uncertainty of the Great Depression.

"He was an idealist," says Castle McLaughlin, who describes her grandfather as a believer who genuinely cared about the sport of hockey, and not the commercial aspect. "He wanted it to succeed, but he was doing it because he was passionate. He could've put his money in a million other things. The whole culture is so different today. People probably couldn't imagine playing in those conditions and trying to keep it going from week to week and year to year."

Standing on the ice that night, McLaughlin was a man who already had accomplished much. After graduating from Harvard in 1901, he eventually became president of his family's coffee company, W.F. McLaughlin Co. During World War I, he commanded 800 men in the U.S. Army's 86th Division (333rd Machine Gun Battalion). McLaughlin had been one of the nation's top polo players, and one of its most eligible bachelors until he married the famous dancer and fashion designer, Irene Castle, in 1923.

The Major loved to win. While stationed at Camp Grant, near Rockford, Illinois, he became invested in the success of its boxing program, offering to pay for a world class instructor when the camp's men were

The 1936–37 Chicago Blackhawks during training camp in Hibbing, Minnesota.
(Photo courtesy of Ty Dilello/Manitoba Hockey Hall of Fame)

Major Frederic McLaughlin and coach Emil Iverson, probably during the 1932–33 season. (SDN-0102868, Chicago Sun-Times/Chicago Daily News collection, Chicago History Museum)

whupped by boxers from Camp Dodge. In 1918, just days after the 86th Division became the Black Hawk Division, McLaughlin was delighted when Camp Grant's boxers won all seven bouts (including six technical knockouts) against Canadian fighters during an Independence Day celebration before 100,000 spectators.

In August 1933, McLaughlin was celebrated for organizing the East-West polo match in his hometown of Lake Forest, Illinois, and proving the nation's Western players could challenge and beat the top Eastern players. As a sportsman and polo aficionado, it may have been hard for him to imagine surpassing the West's victory in what many called the "World Series of polo." Yet, his Blackhawks tasted Stanley Cup glory for the very first time just eight months later.

The Blackhawks' epic brawl with the Maple Leafs captures the sweep and clamor of professional hockey in the 1930s, when life and sport were tough and mean, and charismatic owners like McLaughlin played for keeps. It happened right in between the team's 1934 and 1938 Stanley Cup victories—world championships that illuminated a struggling city during the darkness of the Great Depression.

The Great Depression

Just five months after the stock market crash of October 1929, national unemployment more than doubled to 3.2 million. Compared to roughly 3,000 in 1929, the number of foreclosures in Chicago had surpassed 15,000 by 1933. As the contents of homes were emptied onto neighborhood sidewalks, many evicted residents were forced to live in shelters. An astonishing 40 percent of Chicagoans were jobless in 1932, and those who were employed worked for reduced wages. Between 1934 and 1937 alone, roughly one-third of the city's inhabitants received government assistance. Every day, hundreds scoured city garbage dumps to look for discarded scraps of meat, fruit, and vegetables.

The Depression's sting was less noticeable in wealthier Chicago-area enclaves like Lake Forest, where the McLaughlins lived. In her autobiography, Irene Castle wrote: "The Depression did not affect the residents of Lake Forest to any great extent," noting that when banks began to close, she was in Palm Beach, Florida, and experienced only a minor inconvenience waiting for Frederic to wire money for her return trip. Castle said that most Lake Forest residents faced the Depression by reducing the number of horses in their stables.

Professional hockey players were not immune to the economic fallout. At one point, longtime Blackhawks forward Johnny Gottselig saw his pay reduced by 25 percent. The pay cut likely reflected falling revenues at the gate. Gottselig once explained that game attendance in Chicago had been affected more severely than in other cities where the team played.

Homeless Chicagoans sleep under Michigan Avenue during the Great Depression. (DN-0093220, Chicago Sun-Times/Chicago Daily News collection, Chicago History Museum)

The Great Escape

Sports provided a welcome diversion from everyday reality during this difficult time. The Chicago Bears celebrated championships in both 1932 and 1933. The Chicago Cubs made an appearance in the World Series in 1932 but lost to the New York Yankees in four straight games. The following summer, Chicagoans witnessed the very first Major League Baseball All-Star game at Comiskey Park. Conceived by *Chicago Tribune* sportswriter Arch Ward, the contest—a 4-2 American League victory—was dubbed "the game of the century."

Compared to other professional sports, hockey offered Chicagoans the most exciting escape of all. In a February 17, 1934, *Liberty Magazine* article, Dick Williams described NHL hockey as "that mad, glad, man-smashing epidemic from Canada," and debated its status as a game or an affliction. "This game of hockey hit the United States in a big way at about the same moment as the platinum blonde," he wrote. "It

Events like the Garfield Park Silver Skates speedskating event (1937) were a popular diversion from the Great Depression for participants and spectators alike. (Chicago Park District Records, Photographs, 022_040_024, Special Collections, Chicago Public Library)

has been a question ever since which has caused the more hospital bills and bred the more cardiac trouble among noncombatants. Certainly there are few known cures for hockey addiction in a nonparticipant. . . . They call American football rough. It's pattycake beside a match in the National Hockey League. Human bodies, moving at a speed twice as great as the fastest running halfback achieves, crash together head on, minus helmets of any kind. If they miss one another, they have a chance of fetching up against four-foot-high sideboards."

The mere presence of sports heroes lifted the community's spirits during the darkest of days, and the Blackhawks were no exception. Long before television or social media, public admiration for the players was hard to miss. Joan Karakas, daughter of legendary goalie Mike Karakas, remembers what it was like being the daughter of a big-league athlete in 1930s Chicago, recalling: "Through a young person's eyes, everywhere we went, when you said your last name, they would say, 'Do you have anything to do with Mike Karakas?' I would say, 'That's my daddy.' My mother, my sister, and I, wherever we went, restaurants or shopping, the minute you said your name, it was like he was a big celebrity.

"Of course, life was so different back then because you didn't have television," she continued. "You had radio, but no TV, so when people got to meet you, I think it was a little more exciting for them because these were not people you saw every day, like on a TV screen or anything."

A Different Game

Along with life in general, hockey was different during the 1930s. John Robertson, who joined the Blackhawks as an assistant trainer in 1937 and during the mid-1990s was still guarding the team's locker room door at United Center, once elaborated on how the gear was different for professional players during this era. "Now, everything is plush," he said. "In those days, everything was plain old wooden floors. They didn't have the protective equipment they have today. I mean, you used to have to sew felt on long underwear. You'd go in the dressing room and it would smell like billy goats, because if they were successful in winning, they wouldn't even let you wash their underwear. I can remember when Mush March had a streak going, he refused to wash his underwear and stuff. By the end of the season, it was getting pretty bad."

One of Robertson's early jobs was to run the first-aid room at Chicago Stadium. When tending to injured players from opposing teams, he occasionally cut the laces out of their hockey gloves. This delayed their return to the ice by a few extra minutes.

March, who played right wing for the Blackhawks from 1928 to 1945, once reflected on how the game had evolved since his time as a player. "The game is much faster today, because it has opened up more," he said in 1996. "We could not shoot the puck over the red line or the blue line; we had to carry it in and then pass it." (The NHL added the red line at center ice in 1943–44 to accelerate play and minimize offside calls.)

"It was a tougher game in those days," Johnny Gottselig said in an April 1979 *Hockey* article by Greg Mahoney. "There were only 11 or 12 men to a team then, and it was not unusual for a player to go five or six minutes on a shift. Everyone checked, even the star forwards."

The January 4, 1936, issue of *Collier's* explained how the game had evolved since its formative years: "In the old days it was a question of one team going out and blasting around until the opposition either died or got out of the way. The teams now carry sixteen players, a doctor and several trainers. The trick of the manager is to keep his teams fresh, with the result that to the ordinary spectator an evening of hockey consists of lines of players tumbling over the railing by the bench and rushing into the fray. By alternating three fresh teams, there is no let-up in

John Robertson (left) is pictured with his father, George "Gordon" Robertson (center), and brother Kenneth Gordon Robertson (right) in the trainers' room at Chicago Stadium. All three worked for the Blackhawks in various capacities. Kenneth started as a stick boy, eventually becoming an assistant trainer, while Gordon (also known as "Mr. R") and John spent many years controlling access to dressing rooms for the team and officials. (Photo courtesy of Elizabeth Buzenius)

the pace and no opportunity for a gentleman who enjoys a good nap on the ice."

Jean McKean, daughter of former Blackhawks center Carl "Cully" Dahlstrom, recalls her father's philosophy about settling scores during this era. "One of the things that I remember my dad always saying was that you just really had to be a smart player," she said. "There were fights, just like there are today, if not worse, but he said that you knew you had to get them back and get even, but you had to wait for the right time when they least expected it."

Carl Liscombe, who played left wing for the Detroit Red Wings during the 1930s and 1940s, explained that high-sticking was uncommon during an era when players did not wear helmets or protective face shields and had a mutual interest in avoiding career-ending injuries. "That was an unwritten rule," he said. "Nobody high-sticked back then. If you high-sticked, you didn't touch the puck the rest of the night, I'll tell you, because you had five guys chasing you all night long. That's just a figure of speech, of course, but you kept your head up."

Because goaltenders did not usually wear helmets or masks during the 1930s, playing that position came with additional risks, which was reflected in their style of play. "All goaltenders back in those days were standup goaltenders; they never went down," Liscombe said. "It was a different game altogether. We didn't have the pileups in front of the net like they do now. They didn't have any masks on, either. If they were going down, they were going to get hit."

Like players' salaries, ticket prices also were much lower during the 1930s. In a 1995 interview, the late Tom Gaston—a devoted Hockey Hall of Fame volunteer who began attending Toronto Maple Leafs games during the late 1920s—recalled paying about 60 cents to watch Toronto play the Montreal Maroons in 1928–29. Several years later, he was present for the first game ever played at Maple Leaf Gardens, paying about 80 cents to see March score the very first goal in the historic arena.

Resurfacing the ice was a more cumbersome, manual process in the days before Zambonis. "When I first went down, they didn't flood [the ice] between periods," Gaston said. "In the early days, they flooded it with a hose, with a nozzle on it. I can remember the first time I went in the Gardens, when it was being built, and they were just flooding the ice for the first or second time. They had a big fire hose with a sprayer on it, like a big watering can. That's how they did it; they went back and forth."

Underworld Threats

During the 1930s, the specter of organized crime meant that Chicago could be a scary place for hockey families from smaller American and

Canadian towns. Defenseman Art Coulter once told his daughter that gangsters were very prevalent in the city when he played there. One night, at a restaurant with some teammates, he looked through the window and witnessed someone getting gunned down by another person with a machine gun. In a November 30, 1938, letter, Cully Dahlstrom's wife, Gladys, wrote: "A couple of gangsters had a shooting party in our block last night. They shot a nice policeman and killed him, but one of the cops killed the fellow who shot him."

"My dad said that [gangsters] would hang around the rink in their fedoras and their overcoats, with their chin on their hand, at rinkside, watching everything," recalled Virginia Hansen, daughter of former

This section of a map of Chicago's gangland shows the general area where many Chicago Blackhawks players and their families lived during the 1930s. (Bruce-Roberts, Inc., 1931; retrieved from the Library of Congress)

Doc Romnes and wife Grace with daughter Virginia in 1936. (Photo courtesy of the Doc Romnes family)

Blackhawks forward Elwin "Doc" Romnes. "If, after a game, they would go out for a beer, they never had to buy; they had guys there that would buy for the players."

As several Blackhawks players would discover, the criminal element was dangerously close at times. Although she cannot remember the exact location, Hansen recalls an unsettling episode her mother experienced at one Chicago hotel. "Evidently, somebody had been living there that was connected with the Mafia," she said. "They had been in that same suite. They came and my mother answered the door; I guess my dad wasn't home. They asked for this person and she said, 'I don't know that person; I've never seen them and they don't live here.' They pulled a gun on her and insisted on getting some information."

According to Antonia Chambers's *Before the Echoes Fade*, mobsters approached goaltender Chuck Gardiner during the 1933–34 season. Revealing a briefcase full of cash, they offered to make throwing the occasional game worth his while. Outraged, Gardiner told them to "Go to Hell!" and reported the incident to both his coach and the police. A few weeks later, Gardiner returned home from practice to find his wife, Myrtle, extremely upset. Their son, Bobby, was nowhere to be found. Fearing he had been kidnapped, the Gardiners contacted police, who began a search of speakeasies and other locations frequented by the mob. Although Bobby eventually was found sleeping under his bed, the incident convinced the Gardiners to send Bobby back home to Winnipeg with Marie Couture, the wife of teammate Rosario "Lolo" Couture. Police and federal agents monitored their journey.

Gardiner was not the only Stanley Cup-winning goalie to face pressure from underworld figures during the 1930s. A letter to Mike Karakas, pasted in the late netminder's scrapbook, prompted his daughter Joan to recall how mobsters once tried to influence Iron Mike's performance, quite possibly during the Stanley Cup playoffs.

"The story he told is that these were Al Capone's men, and they wanted him to throw a game," she recalled. "I get the feeling that it was a big game, like the Stanley Cup. According to what my father said, naturally he was kind of scared and nervous. You didn't want to get fresh with these guys or anything, but he tried to tell them that with hockey, it's too fast a game; you couldn't throw it even if you wanted to. So they took him for a ride and they roughed him up a little bit.

"From what I can remember, back in those days he had a really nice expensive Sheaffer fountain pen and a watch," she continued. "They all had engravings, because these were things from fans, with his name on it. They took all the stuff and threw it out, and then they threw him out of the car. He said he was pretty scared. My father wasn't a big talker; he was a man of few words, but he said, 'I just tried to tell them, even if I wanted to, I couldn't.' He was very honest, so they had to teach him a lesson."

Bright Moments

While times were tough during the 1930s, Chicago was not without excitement. The city celebrated its 100th birthday in 1933 with the Century of Progress International Exposition (the World's Fair), which opened on May 27 and operated for two years. The fair attracted approximately

39 million people who paid 50 cents to escape the Great Depression, if only for a little while. Held on more than 400 acres of land in Northerly Park, which later became Meigs Field, the event included futuristic buildings and exhibits devoted to achievements in transportation, science, and industry, along with carnivalesque attractions like freak shows, dancing fleas, and Free Beer Day.

McLaughlin's family did not hesitate to enjoy the fair's many attractions. In 1933, one newspaper ran a photo depicting Irene Castle with her children, nine-year-old Barbara and five-year-old William, enjoying an amusement ride. After returning to Chicago from Canada for the start of the 1933–34 season, Blackhawks goaltender Chuck Gardiner took his family to the fair as well, enjoying rides with Bobby, entertaining fans by singing songs, and appearing on an experimental version of television.

CHAPTER 2

Working Class Heroes

lthough many NHL players were adored by fans during the 1930s, their lifestyles more closely mirrored those of the working class, and not big celebrities. Cully Dahlstrom, the NHL's top rookie in 1937–38, earned a starting salary of $4,000 that supported a relatively simple existence. In a 1936 article he wrote for *American Legion Monthly*, Frederic McLaughlin described how much money NHL players then earned. "Hockey salaries are liberal, but not extravagant," he said, explaining that NHL rookies typically made $3,000 per year in 1936 (the equivalent of $56,457 in 2021), while the average NHL salary was $4,800 ($90,331). Team payrolls averaged $75,000 ($1.41 million).

"I played 17 years, and I made about $85,000," Harold "Mush" March recalled in 1996. "These guys today are making millions in one year. I guess the good Lord was looking after me anyway. It was a different time. In those days, they weren't paying you much. I think if you made $10,000, you had a good job. I think Howie Morenz probably made that, and [Toronto's Charlie] Conacher, and [New York's Frank] Boucher, and [Boston's] Eddie Shore."

Getting to work was easy for Blackhawks players during the late 1930s—even the ones who could not afford their own car. "We stayed at the Guyon Hotel," said Dahlstrom. "Some of the team had connections in Chicago [and] lived in different places. But most of us, we single ones and some married ones, too, stayed at the Guyon Hotel. It was about

Mush March pumps gas in 1934. (SDN-076440, Chicago Sun-Times/Chicago Daily News collection, Chicago History Museum)

three quarters of a mile from the Stadium, so it was reasonably close for us. We always could get a bus and go down to the rink, until we finally got cars."

Garfield Park

The Guyon Hotel was in the Garfield Park area of Chicago. The recreation area of the same name, with its lagoon and conservatory, is between the West Garfield Park and East Garfield Park neighborhoods, beyond which Chicago Stadium was located on the Near West Side. Many Blackhawks players and their families lived in this area during the 1930s and 1940s, not only at the Guyon Hotel but also locations like the Midwest Athletic Club.

According to the Chicago Recreation Commission's *Local Community Fact Book* 1938, during the mid-1930s about 46,650 people lived in West Garfield Park, which it described as "one of Chicago's busiest and most densely populated outlying sections." West Garfield Park included the Guyon Hotel, Madison-Crawford Shopping Center, Legler Branch Library, Washington Boulevard Temple, St. Mel's High School, Mid-

The Guyon Hotel. (Photo courtesy of the Virgil Johnson family)

HOTEL GUYON—"THE HOME OF HOMES"—4000 WASHINGTON BLVD., CHICAGO, ILL.

Postcard from the Guyon Hotel. (Photo courtesy of the Cully Dahlstrom family)

Rough and tumble Chicago defensemen Art Wiebe (left) and Earl Seibert (right) enjoy a softer moment on the ice by teaching Art's daughter, four-year-old Diane Marilyn Wiebe, how to ice skate in Chicago's Garfield Park. (Photo courtesy of the Art Wiebe family)

west Athletic Club, and Robert Burns Hospital. The population consisted mainly of Jews, Slavs, and Italians. Another 56,563 people lived in East Garfield Park, which was home to Sears Roebuck, a YMCA, the Ballington Booth Community Center, the 132nd Infantry Armory, Little Jack's Restaurant, and the Graemere Hotel. Like West Garfield Park, the neighborhood included many Italians and Jews, as well as Irish and Russian residents.

Both neighborhoods mainly consisted of businesses and multiple-family apartments, including two-flats and small apartment buildings. There was no shortage of things to do on either side of the lagoon. West Garfield Park included two public playgrounds and one branch library, a ballroom, four "fifth class" halls, two dancing schools, seven liquor establishments with dance music, 110 traditional liquor establishments, seven motion picture theaters, and one mechanical riding device. East Garfield Park offered a similar mix of entertainment options, including a bowling alley, five motion picture theaters, and 142 liquor establishments.

Family Life

A letter from Helen Johnson, the wife of Blackhawks defenseman Virgil Johnson, to Virgil's mother, Agnes, on December 16, 1943, provides a glimpse of what life was like for players and their families at the Guyon Hotel around this general time. "We have a one room apartment to live in and I like it a lot," she wrote. "However, they have put our name on the waiting list for an apartment with a bedroom, as they are only $1.00 more a week, and it will be better for Johnny [their son, Virgil Charles (Johnny)] than sleeping on the davenport. The apartment has a real nice kitchen, large enough for Johnny and me to eat in."

Another letter, written several months later, described the closeness that existed between some of the hockey families at the hotel: "After the game, I had a surprise birthday party for Virg up in the Dahlstrom apartment," wrote Helen. "We played games and I served cold

Cully Dahlstrom's daughter, Ruth, and Virgil Johnson's son, Virgil C. Johnson, pose for a photo in 1944. (Photo courtesy of the Virgil Johnson family)

Blackhawks defenseman Art Wiebe (left) and his wife, Mary Ann (right), pose for a picture on a winter day in Chicago. (Photo courtesy of the Art Wiebe family)

Earl Seibert gives a toy doll to Art Wiebe's daughter, Diane, while celebrating Christmas in the Guyon Hotel. (Photo courtesy of the Art Wiebe family)

fried chicken, potato salad, coleslaw and hard rolls. The ten of us ate twelve pounds of chicken. Virgil got some wonderful birthday presents and won't have to buy a thing for ages."

In a letter to his parents, likely written during the early 1940s, Virgil Johnson added: "We do our own cooking here and it's much cheaper than eating out every day. Yesterday I bought a chicken and Earl Seibert cooked it in a pressure cooker and it was really good. So you see we don't starve."

In the same letter, Johnson described how he and four teammates went bowling with Eddie Shipstad, Henry (Heinie) Brock, and other members of the Ice Follies touring ice show. "They beat us of course, but I never bowl," he wrote. "Even then I did fairly well."

Mark Hemstock, grandson of defenseman Art Wiebe, recalled his grandfather's friendship with fellow blueliner, Earl Seibert. In the December 24, 1982, issue of the *Hockey News*, he described how Seibert frequented his grandparents' Guyon Hotel apartment. "Earl was always spoiling my mother—feeding her ginger-ale, popsicles and candy," he said.

Art Wiebe (center) and Earl Seibert (right) enjoy a drink with a friend in 1942. (Photo courtesy of the Art Wiebe family)

Mr. and Mrs. Paul Thompson at home in 1933. (SDN-074182, Chicago Sun-Times/ Chicago Daily News collection, Chicago History Museum)

On February 2, 1936, the *Chicago Sunday Tribune* published a series of photos that captured the personal lives of Blackhawks players during the 1930s. One shows goaltender Mike Karakas and forward Tom Cook wearing fedoras, neckties, and dress coats. The men, who had recently become fathers, were carrying an assortment of non-hockey equipment, including a doll, stuffed animal, tricycle, and baby carriage. Other players, all looking very dapper in dress shirts, ties, and vests, engaged in a variety of activities during an afternoon off. Marty Burke, Glenn Brydson (smoking a pipe) and Earl Seibert played billiards. Mush March, Louis Trudel, and Alex Levinsky (also smoking a pipe) enjoyed a hand of bridge. Bowling was the choice of Art Wiebe, Paul Thompson, and Bill Kendall.

During the grind of the regular hockey season, close bonds developed between the players' wives and families. At home, the hockey wives looked after each other's children. Having a strong social network was an advantage in a big city like Chicago.

According to letters written by Cully Dahlstrom's wife, Gladys, to her mother, Sadie Erwin, and her sister, Helen, the girls frequented movie theaters, played bridge in each other's apartments, and shopped at downtown Chicago stores like Marshall Field's. Sometimes, they enjoyed tea at Ruby's, within the Graemere Hotel. Located at Homan Avenue and Washington Boulevard, the Graemere was situated across from Garfield Park and, like the Guyon, included permanent residents.

Some of the hockey wives joined the Midwest Athletic Club in West Garfield Park, where they took swing and tap-dancing lessons, played badminton, and enjoyed swimming and steam baths. According to a nomination form for the National Register of Historic Places, prepared in 1983 by freelance architectural historian Susan S. Benjamin, the building "was the focus of community life in Garfield Park."

Benjamin's report provided a glimpse into the tightknit West Side community where the players and their families lived and worked. "The Club was a vital part of the community, and remained so, if on a smaller scale, after the Depression," it explained. "Even before the building was constructed, in 1926, a women's auxiliary was formed and at one point, had 450 members. It sponsored social events and had, in the building,

Wives of Chicago Blackhawks players, wearing team jackets, socialize outside the Graemere Hotel during the 1930s. (Photo courtesy of the Art Wiebe family)

its own dining room and lounge; from the beginning, the club was not just to be a luncheon club for men."

When the Blackhawks were at home, their families were frequently treated to meals and entertainment. "Tonight we are all going to the ice carnival as guests of someone," Gladys Dahlstrom wrote in a November 22, 1938, letter. "It's nice to go to things for free. The boys get passes to a lot of things."

In addition to going out on the town and being treated to elaborate dancing and dinner engagements, Chicago's hockey families enjoyed many simple times together, playing games like Chinese checkers and ping-pong on the second floor of the Guyon Hotel and gathering for late-night sandwiches in their apartments after games. "It was a different time," said Cully Dahlstrom's daughter, Jean McKean. "Those families got together, and all those little children got together. These big guys were dads and husbands. They did a lot of things together."

When they were not eating home-cooked meals, players like Earl Seibert (left) and Virgil Johnson (right) enjoyed going out on the town. Mary Ann Wiebe, wife of defenseman Art Wiebe, is seated to Johnson's left. (Photo courtesy of the Art Wiebe family)

Hockey players and their families make time for an outing in 1941. Chicago Blackhawks teammates Cully Dahlstrom and Virgil Johnson appear far left and far right, respectively. (Photo courtesy of the Cully Dahlstrom family)

Mary Ann Wiebe, wife of defenseman Art Wiebe, uses a movie camera near the Guyon Hotel. (Photo courtesy of the Art Wiebe family)

Chicago players and their families near the Guyon Hotel during the 1930s, apparently after some recreational ice skating. Cully Dahlstrom (far right) is holding daughter Ruth, accompanied by his wife, Gladys Ruth Erwin Dahlstrom, who wears a team jacket. (Photo courtesy of the Art Wiebe family)

Two "Blue Goose" streetcars are seen at Madison and Central in 1937. A boxy trolley bus is visible on Central. Madison Street divides Chicago's North and South Sides and is one of the city's oldest transit streets. (Photo courtesy of Chicago Transit Authority)

Getting Around

During the grit and grime of the Depression, locals and hockey transplants made their way around the city in different ways. While Dahlstrom and his teammates sometimes took the bus, a few had automobiles. Streetcars were an especially popular means of transportation—especially near Chicago Stadium. During the 1930s, thousands of electric streetcars traversed hundreds of Chicago streets.

Players and fans alike could reach the Stadium on one of 83 Presidents Conference Committee (PCC) streetcars that eventually operated on the Madison Street Line. Dubbed the "Blue Goose" because of its streamlined appearance and color scheme (blue and cream with a red center band), the PCC was developed in response to the Depression's negative impact on public transportation. To rectify the situation, industry leaders collectively designed the larger PCC cars, two of which were used experimentally during the 1934 World's Fair.

The first PCC cars appeared during a nighttime transit pageant on November 12, 1936. An estimated 500,000 people stood on both sides

The Chicago Transit Authority's Madison Street Station House was used until 1951 and functioned as a hot dog stand through the 1980s. (Photo courtesy of Bruce Moffat/Chicago Transit Authority)

of Madison Street, from the Loop to the city limits, to celebrate their arrival. Costing $16,000 each, they seated 58 people and had a balancing speed of 42 mph. Public displays appeared the following day at State and Adams and State and Madison when the cars officially entered service.

In addition to streetcars, the "L" train was among the best ways to reach Blackhawks games during the 1930s. The Madison Street Station, located at the Stadium, connected the arena to the rest of the city. According to the Chicago Transit Authority's Bruce Moffat, the Madison Street Station House was used until 1951. The platforms were removed sometime between 1966 and 1968, and the structure functioned as a hot dog stand through the 1980s. During the early 2020s, the tracks remained an active portion of CTA's Pink Line.

1933-34
STANLEY
CUP

When President Franklin Delano Roosevelt visited the World's Fair on October 2, 1933, Chicagoans were anticipating the start of another hockey season. The city had nearly tasted Stanley Cup glory in 1930–31, when coach Dick Irvin led the Blackhawks to a second-place American Division finish (24-17-3, 51 points). However, the team was eliminated in the finals by the Montreal Canadiens, who won the best-of-five series 3-2. In 1931–32, Chicago finished second in the American Division with an 18-19-11 (47 points) record and was defeated by the Toronto Maple Leafs in the quarterfinals.

Although the Blackhawks slipped to fourth place in the American Division in 1932–33, finishing 16-20-12 (44 points) and failing to make the playoffs, Chicago had a new coach in Tommy Gorman, who joined the team mid-season. Gorman knew a thing or two about winning hockey championships, having managed the Ottawa Senators to three Stanley Cup victories during the early 1920s. He remained behind the bench in 1933–34 as the Blackhawks prepared to make a run for professional hockey's ultimate prize.

The 1932–33 Chicago Blackhawks, pictured with Coach Emil Iverson, featured players who contributed to the team's Stanley Cup victories in both 1933–34 and 1937–38, including Art Wiebe, Louis Trudel, Doc Romnes, Art Coulter, Don McFadyen, Johnny Gottselig, Roger Jenkins, Paul Thompson, Taffy Abel, Lolo Couture, Chuck Gardiner, Tommy Cook, and Mush March. (Photo courtesy of Ty Dilello/Manitoba Hockey Hall of Fame)

1933-34 Chicago Blackhawks

Name	Position	Games	Goals	Assists	Points	Penalty Minutes
Clarence Abel	D	46	2	1	3	28
Lionel Conacher	D	48	10	13	23	87
Tom Cook	C	37	5	9	14	15
Art Coulter	D	41	5	2	7	39
Thomas Coulter	F	2	0	0	0	0
Rosie Couture	RW	48	5	8	13	21
Duke Dukowski	F/D	5	0	0	0	2
Charlie Gardiner (C)	G	48	1.63 GAA	0	0	0
Leroy Goldsworthy	RW	27	3	3	6	0
Johnny Gottselig	LW	48	16	14	30	4
Roger Jenkins	RW/D	48	2	2	4	37
Bill Kendall	RW	21	3	0	3	0
Jack Leswick	F	37	1	7	8	16
Harold March	RW	48	4	13	17	26
Don McFadyen	F	34	1	3	4	20
Elwin Romnes	LW/C	47	8	21	29	6
Johnny Sheppard	C	38	3	4	7	4
Paul Thompson	LW	48	20	16	36	17
Louis Trudel	LW	34	1	3	4	13

*Regular season statistics. Source: Chicago Blackhawks

CHAPTER 3

The Great Contenders

L ed by coach Tommy Gorman, Chicago's first Stanley Cup team included several standout players, like Clarence "Taffy" Abel, Lionel "Big Train" Conacher, Art Coulter, Charles "Chuck" Gardiner, Johnny Gottselig, Harold "Mush" March, Elwin "Doc" Romnes, and Paul Thompson.

Thomas Patrick "Tommy" Gorman

Born on June 9, 1886, Tommy Gorman was named head coach of the Blackhawks in 1932–33. After piloting the team through the season's final 25 games, he remained behind the bench in 1933–34. Gorman first made his mark on the sports world as a lacrosse player, winning the 1908 Olympic Games First Prize in London, England, as a member of the Canadian Lacrosse Team. Like his father, he was a sports reporter for the *Ottawa Citizen*, but gave up newspaper work in 1921 to pursue a sports promotion and management career.

Gorman became one of the NHL's founders when he and Ted Dey purchased the Ottawa Hockey Association, whose owners were going to let it lapse. A friend loaned him half of the $5,000 asking price. When hockey exploded in popularity after World War I, Gorman sold

---

(opposite) Tommy Gorman in October 1933. (SDN-075368, Chicago Sun-Times/ Chicago Daily News collection, Chicago History Museum)

Chicago "Black Hawks"---Stanley Cup Winners, Year 1934
Emblematic of World's Professional Championship
LEFT TO RIGHT — THE LATE CHUCK GARDINER, TOMMY COOK, ROGER JENKINS, LOLA COUTURE, PAUL THOMPSON, JOHNNY GOTTSELIG, LIONEL CONACHER, ART COULTER, TOMMY GORMAN, TAFFY ABEL, DOC ROMNES, LOUIS TRUDELL, JACK LESWICK, MUSH MARSH, JOHNNY McFADDEN, BILL KENDAL, JOE STARK.

(CCM Skates photo courtesy of the Chuck Gardiner family)

his ownership stake to Frank Ahearn for $35,000 and Ahearn's interest in the Connaught Park Jockey Club.

Gorman managed the Ottawa Senators to Stanley Cups in 1919–20, 1920–21, and 1922–23 with coach Pete Green. One of his most memorable coaching moments happened behind the Chicago bench on March 14, 1933, during a game against the Boston Bruins. In overtime, the Boston team swarmed around Chicago's goal in an aggressive scoring attempt. This resulted in a goal at 3:13 by Bruins center Marty Barry, but Gorman claimed the goal light was lit before the puck went into the net.

Outraged, Chicago forward Johnny Gottselig attempted to strike goal umpire Louis Raycroft with his stick. After restoring order, referee Bill Stewart proceeded to have the teams face off at center ice, but Gorman called him over to the Chicago bench to protest the goal. Gorman allegedly punched Stewart in the face, provoking a fight that was broken up by the Boston team. Stewart had Gorman, under protest, removed to the Blackhawks' dressing room by police. When the coach ordered his team to follow, Stewart ruled the game a forfeit, giving Boston a 1-0 victory.

"Tommy Gorman knew psychology," Blackhawks defenseman Art Coulter recalled in a 1989 interview with author Antonia Chambers. "He promised he would get raises for things like making All-Star, winning the Stanley Cup. After we won the Cup, I went to Major McLaughlin and asked for my raise. He called Gorman, and Gorman confirmed what he had said. So I got the raise; I think I was the only one. Gorman once said to him, 'Money is the only tool I got.'"

Clarence John "Taffy" Abel

Standing at 6'1" and weighing up to 235 pounds during his career, Taffy Abel was a sizable presence on defense. The Sault Ste. Marie, Michigan, native was the first American-born hockey player to win the Stanley Cup. He also was the first American Indian, according to a March/April 2013 *Michigan History* article by Bill Castanier and Gregory Parker, which explained that his heritage (Abel's grandfather was a member of the Chippewa tribe) was not widely known.

Abel did not play organized hockey until he was 18 years old. After playing at the amateur level, he became a defenseman in the Thunder Bay Senior Hockey League (TBSHL), playing for the Michigan Soo Nationals in 1918–19 and the Michigan Soo Wildcats from 1919–22, where he established a reputation as a physical player. Abel then suited up for the United States Amateur Hockey Association's (USAHA) St. Paul Athletic Club, where he played from 1922–25.

Abel carried the American flag in Chamonix, France, in 1924 as a member of the U.S. Olympic team during the first Winter Games. There, he took the Olympic oath for hockey players. Although Canada beat the United States 6-1, Abel scored 15 goals in five games and was celebrated as an Olympic hero in his hometown of Sault Ste. Marie.

Castanier and Gregory explained that Abel's nickname, Taffy, stemmed from his affection for the candy, which he would sneak into school during his youth. Popular with crowds, his towering size resulted in a mix of other nicknames, including Michigan Mountain, Stonewall, Pachyderm, and Mack Truck.

Taffy went pro with the Central Hockey League's (CHL) Minneapolis Millers in 1925–26 and broke into the NHL as one of the original New

Clarence John "Taffy" Abel

Birthplace:	Sault Ste. Marie, Michigan
Born:	May 28, 1900
Died:	August 1, 1964
Position:	Defense
Weight:	223
Height:	6'1"
Chicago Blackhawks Stats	
Uniform #:	2
Games Played:	223
Goals:	8
Assists:	12
Points:	20
Penalty Minutes:	212
Seasons:	1929–34
Career Awards & Honors	
U.S. Hockey Hall of Fame:	1973
Upper Peninsula Sports Hall of Fame:	1972
American Indian Athletic Hall of Fame:	1989

York Rangers in 1926–27, helping the club win its first Stanley Cup in 1928. When injury sidelined Rangers goaltender Lorne Chabot during the finals that year, 45-year-old manager and coach Lester Patrick took his place. Because Patrick had no NHL goaltending experience, this put extra pressure on Taffy and defenseman Ivan "Ching" Johnson.

The Blackhawks paid $15,000 for Abel's contract in April 1929. That year, the *Los Angeles Times* ranked him as the heaviest hockey player in the world, according to *Michigan History*. Abel remained in the Windy City for five seasons, becoming a fan favorite. After a contract dispute with the Blackhawks ended his career, he coached several hockey teams in Sault Ste. Marie, where he ran the Log Cabin Cafe and the Log Cabin Lodge on Ashmun Street, which featured several cabins. A heart attack claimed Abel's life in 1964. In 2012, the Smithsonian Institution's Na-

---

(opposite) Taffy Abel enjoys a lighthearted moment with Boston opponent Eddie Shore in 1935. (SDN-076930, Chicago Sun-Times/Chicago Daily News collection, Chicago History Museum)

tional Museum of the American Indian included him in a Native Olympians exhibit.

Lionel Pretoria "Big Train" Conacher

One of 10 children, defenseman Lionel Conacher was born into poverty. Although he dropped out of school after the eighth grade to help support his family, he ultimately found success through exceptional athletic prowess that made him one of the world's greatest all-around athletes. Conacher was named Canada's Athlete of the Half Century (1901–50) for his abilities in eight different sports, including hockey, football, lacrosse, boxing, baseball, wrestling, swimming, and track.

The December 30, 1950, *Calgary Herald* described Conacher as "almost a one-man show in football. He was better-than-average in lacrosse, baseball, hockey, boxing, wrestling, sculling, swimming and track. There isn't much doubt he could have scaled the heights in all had there been more than 24 hours in a day. Endowed with a powerful physique and almost-phenomenal endurance, he sometimes participated in two separate sports in a space of hours."

In 1921, his first year playing senior football, Conacher led the Toronto Argonauts in a 23-0 rout over the Edmonton Eskimos. In the International Professional Lacrosse League, he was a star player for the Montreal Maroons. As a baseball player, he played for the AAA Toronto Maple Leafs of the International League, which won the Little World Series in 1926. As a boxer, Conacher ranked as Canada's light-heavyweight boxing champion and went four rounds with heavyweight champion Jack Dempsey in an exhibition match.

Conacher was a relative latecomer to ice hockey and did not learn to skate until age 16 on a schoolyard rink near his home. Despite this, the Montreal Canadiens offered him a $5,000 professional contract six years later, though he turned it down. Between 1916–17 and 1922–23, Conacher played for several junior and senior teams in the Toronto area, including the Toronto Century Rovers, Toronto Aura Lee, Park-

(opposite) Lionel Conacher in the Boston Garden locker room in 1937. (Photo courtesy of the Boston Public Library, Leslie Jones Collection)

Lionel Pretoria "Big Train" Conacher

Birthplace:	Toronto, Ontario
Born:	May 24, 1900
Died:	May 26, 1954
Position:	Defense
Weight:	195
Height:	6'2"
Chicago Blackhawks Stats	
Uniform #:	3
Games Played:	48
Goals:	10
Assists:	13
Points:	23
Penalty Minutes:	87
Seasons:	1933–34
Career Awards & Honors	
All-Star (First Team):	1933–34
Hockey Hall of Fame:	1994
Canada's Sports Hall of Fame:	1955
Ontario Sports Hall of Fame:	1996
Canadian Lacrosse Hall of Fame:	1966
Canadian Football Hall of Fame:	1963

dale Canoe Club, Toronto Canoe Club, and the North Toronto Athletic Association.

After suiting up for the USAHA's Pittsburgh Yellowjackets in 1923, where he remained for two seasons, Conacher began playing in the NHL with the Pittsburgh Pirates in 1925–26. Following nine games with Pittsburgh the next season, he was traded to the New York Americans, remaining there through 1929–30. In November 1930 Conacher was traded to the Montreal Maroons, where he spent six of his remaining seven NHL seasons.

After three years in Montreal, Conacher was traded to the Blackhawks for Teddy Graham in October 1933. The 1933–34 season would be his only one in the Windy City. Besides being an excellent defenseman, Conacher contributed in the scoring department, accumulating 23 points in 48 games for the Blackhawks and tasting Stanley Cup victory for the first, but not last, time.

In October 1934, the Blackhawks traded Conacher back to the Maroons, who won the Stanley Cup that year. In the May 27, 1954, *Ottawa Journal*, Tommy Gorman, who coached both winning teams (Chicago and Montreal), credited Conacher for engineering the two championships. Describing him as "the greatest hockey player I ever handled," Gorman said: "He was grand in every respect, on and off the field or ice. They'll never be another Conacher. He was Canada's greatest."

Several of Conacher's former opponents praised his commitment to the game and style of play in the May 27, 1954, *Lethbridge Herald*. "Lionel Conacher was a great all round athlete, and a clean and honest hockey player who never tried to hurt small players such as myself," recalled Montreal Canadiens star Aurel Joliat. Detroit Red Wings defenseman Wilfred "Bucko" McDonald added: "He played the game from the first drop of the puck to the end. He played it hard, rugged but fair."

When his athletic career ended, Conacher had sustained eight fractures and taken more than 600 stitches from different injuries. After sports, he became a politician in 1937 and was elected to the Ontario legislature for Toronto-Bracondale. Sadly, on May 26, 1954, during an annual softball game between the Press Gallery and members of Parliament, Conacher collapsed and died shortly thereafter, just two days after his 54th birthday.

Arthur Edmund Coulter

One of the most fearsome defensemen of the 1930s, Art Coulter learned to play hockey at The Forks, where the frozen Assiniboine and Red Rivers converged and the action involved "300 kids and one puck," according to the October 20, 2000, *New York Times*. Coulter eventually advanced from river hockey to Winnipeg's City and District Senior Hockey Leagues (City Sr.), playing for the Winnipeg Pilgrims, who won the Manitoba Juvenile Hockey Championship in 1926–27. After his family relocated to Pittsburgh in 1927 to grow their automotive and hardware business, Coulter turned professional with the Canadian-American Hockey League's (Can-Am) Philadelphia Arrows in 1929, where he spent nearly three seasons.

Coulter joined the Blackhawks in February 1932. In the Windy City,

Arthur Edmund Coulter

Birthplace:	Winnipeg, Manitoba
Born:	May 31, 1909
Died:	October 14, 2000
Position:	Defense
Weight:	185
Height:	5'11"
Chicago Blackhawks Stats	
Uniform #:	17, 18
Games Played:	178
Goals:	12
Assists:	15
Points:	27
Penalty Minutes:	211
Seasons:	1931–36
Career Awards & Honors:	
All-Star (Second Team):	1934–35, 1937–38, 1938–39, 1939–40
Hockey Hall of Fame:	1974
Manitoba Hockey Hall of Fame:	1985
Manitoba Sports Hall of Fame:	2009

he was a fixture on defense until January 1936, when a trade sent him to the New York Rangers in exchange for Earl Seibert. In the same *New York Times* article, Coulter claimed that he was traded for talking back to Frederic McLaughlin after the Blackhawks' owner berated some of the players in the locker room. Coulter led the NHL in penalties (90 minutes) in 1937–38, ahead of Toronto's Red Horner (82 minutes), and played in the 1939 NHL All-Star game.

Although some sources claim he never played in an NHL game, the *Chicago Blackhawks Media Guide* credits Art's brother, defenseman Thomas "Tommy" Coulter, for playing in two Blackhawks contests in 1933–34. According to a 2016 Society for International Hockey Research article by James Milks, Tom competed for the 1932 Canadian Olympic team in Los Angeles, in the 440-yard hurdle event, but was disqualified for knocking down four hurdles. After earning an engineering degree at Carnegie Tech, Tom wanted to pursue a graduate economics degree at the University of Chicago but was short on funds during the Great De-

Bill MacKenzie, Baldy Northcott, and Art Coulter pose for a photo outside Baldy Northcott's Sporting Goods in Winnipeg. (Photo courtesy of Ty Dilello/Manitoba Hockey Hall of Fame)

pression. Art suggested that Tom try out for the Blackhawks, explaining that his roommate, Don McFadyen, was funding his University of Chicago Law School education by playing for the team.

Aside from some pickup hockey at Carnegie Tech, it had been nearly a decade since Tom played organized hockey, according to Milks's article. His successful tryout yielded a $2,500 contract, but he was sent to the minors for further development after playing in two games. After skating through a full 47-game season for the American Hockey Association's (AHA) Oklahoma City Warriors in 1933–34, and taking university classes during the spring and summer, Tom attended the Blackhawks' training camp in the fall of 1934, joining his brother on defense. However, he broke his fibula in a collision with former Canadiens star Howie Morenz, who was then on Chicago's roster.

Tom recovered enough to play six games for the Cleveland Falcons (IAHL) in 1934–35, but the injury had taken its toll. Although he later played for St. George of the New South Wales Ice Hockey Association

Brothers Art and Tom Coulter, both wearing Chicago Blackhawks sweaters, battle for the puck during practice. (SDN-076734, Chicago Sun-Times/Chicago Daily News collection, Chicago History Museum)

while living in Australia, Tom's future was in business. After earning a second graduate degree in business administration, his career included stints with Armco and the Chicago Association of Commerce and Industry. Milks's article describes photographs of Tom, who died on December 17, 2003, with President John F. Kennedy, Queen Elizabeth II, Prince Philip, and Canadian Prime Minister John Diefenbaker.

Possessing incredible endurance, strength, and team spirit, Art Coulter was a natural leader. However, in his later years he did not think highly of contemporary hockey pros. As the New York Rangers chased the Stanley Cup in 1994, ultimately winning it for the first time in 54 seasons, seven surviving players from the 1940 team were interviewed. Coulter told the *New York Times* that modern players "just shoot the puck and chase it around like headless chickens." Praising his former teammates and future Hall of Famers for their stickhandling and passing abilities, he said: "Our old team that won the Stanley Cup could skate backwards blindfolded and whup the Rangers they've got today."

After Coulter's last season in New York (1941–42), he became a U.S. citizen and joined the Coast Guard during World War II. Although his professional career came to an end, he continued playing for the Coast Guard Cutters, who competed in the Eastern Hockey League (EHL) in 1942–43 and played a non-league season in 1943–44. After hockey, Coulter ran hardware and importing businesses in Miami, Florida. He died in an Alabama retirement home at age 92.

Charles Robert "Chuck" Gardiner

Charles "Chuck" Gardiner stands out among the NHL's most legendary goalies. After coming to Winnipeg from Scotland at age seven and learning to skate in neighborhood rinks, Gardiner decided to become a netminder because he was not a very fast skater. "We used to flood the back yards of all the homes and improvise hockey teams," he said in a December 3, 1932, *Chicago Daily News* article by John Carmichael. "I couldn't skate very fast, so by unanimous consent I was shoved into the goal and told to stay there. You see, I didn't learn to skate until after I was eight years old.

"I remember the fellows using old magazines as shin pads, wrapping them around their legs, inside the stockings," he continued. "Newspapers—bundles of 'em—would be converted into kidney pads or for whatever purposes the individual needed them. We all wore stocking caps, or toques as we call them, for open air play. Sometimes it would get so cold that we could only stand to play ten minutes at a time. Then we'd go into a near-by shack and warm up by the heat of an old wood stove and go back and finish the period. It was the only way we could survive."

Gardiner began playing for the Winnipeg Midget League's Victorias at age 13. At the midget level, he also played for the Senators before advancing to the juvenile Assiniboine team. At 16, Gardiner was no longer of age to play lower-level hockey. With established goaltenders already in place on local junior teams, he played pickup hockey and filled in as a substitute for other teams whenever he could, ultimately securing a regular spot with the Manitoba Junior Hockey League's (MJHL) Winnipeg Tigers.

Charles Robert "Chuck" Gardiner

Birthplace:	Edinburgh, Scotland
Born:	December 31, 1904
Died:	June 13, 1934
Position:	Goaltender
Weight:	176
Height:	6'
Chicago Blackhawks Stats	
Uniform #:	1
Games Played:	316
Goals Against Average:	2.02
Shutouts:	42
Penalty Minutes:	2
Seasons:	1927–34
Team Captain:	1933–34
Career Awards & Honors	
All-Star (First Team):	1930–31, 1931–32, 1933–34
All-Star (Second Team):	1932–33
Awards:	Vezina Trophy (Most Valuable Goaltender) (1931–32, 1933–34)
Hockey Hall of Fame:	1945
International Hockey Hall of Fame:	1945
Canada's Sports Hall of Fame:	1975
Manitoba Hockey Hall of Fame:	1985
Manitoba Sports Hall of Fame:	1989

Gardiner played for the Tigers from 1921–22 to 1923–24 and advanced to the Manitoba Senior Hockey League's Selkirk Fishermen in 1924–25. He turned pro with the Winnipeg Maroons in 1925–26 but left the AHA club in an April 1927 trade with the Blackhawks, who paid $17,500 for Gardiner, Nick Wasnie, and Cecil Browne. Although Gardiner originally was intended to be a backup goalie for Hugh Lehman, he quickly became the team's top netminder. In Chicago, teammate Duke Keats provided Gardiner with insight that was useful in understanding the moves of forwards on opposing teams.

In addition to his exceptional goaltending skills, Gardiner was a natural leader. On the ice, he was adept at directing his teammates during games. Team owner Frederic McLaughlin took notice of these

Chuck Gardiner at the Winnipeg Amphitheater while playing for the Winnipeg Maroons Hockey Club. (Photo courtesy of the Chuck Gardiner family)

skills and named Gardiner team captain on November 6, 1933. He set an example with his dependability, playing every minute of every game from 1928–29 to 1933–34 and standing out among the league's goaltenders during those six seasons. Even when the Blackhawks were losing, Gardiner's spirit was unbreakable.

Gardiner was a sprawling netminder who often rushed out of the

(Photo courtesy of the Chuck Gardiner family)

net to cut down the angle of opposing forwards. Nicknamed the "Roving Scotsman," he was among the very first goaltenders to use this technique. Gardiner's evolution into a roving goalie happened after his arrival in Chicago.

Murray Murdoch, a former teammate of Gardiner's with the Winnipeg Maroons, also played against him in the NHL as a member of the New York Rangers. "When he went to the Blackhawks, his goaltending style changed," he explained in a 1989 interview with Antonia Chambers. "He developed a whole new goaltending style—coming out of the net to meet the attacker—very effective. It's all in the timing. If you go at someone's feet when they are being chased down from behind it's very hard to change direction. No goalie was using that style. At that time some people said it wouldn't work but we knew. He was very hard to score on."

In *The Chicago Black Hawks Story* by George Vass, Francis "King" Clancy said: "Charlie had everything, sure hands, good eyes, quick reflexes, no weak spots, and a fine team spirit. In his last season of 48 games, 10 of them were shutouts."

"Charlie was one of the best goalkeepers I ever saw," recalled the late Tom Gaston, a longtime Hockey Hall of Fame volunteer, during a 1995 interview. "He was a stand-up, good-natured guy. I think he was the first goalkeeper ever to be a team captain. I admired him very much. I thought he was one of the best, if not the best, goalkeeper of his time—even though his career was short."

Gardiner was a competitive person who hated to lose or be scored on, even in practice. Away from hockey, he ranked as one of the best trap shooters in Canada and was an excellent baseball and rugby player. Gardiner also had an interest in business and owned his own sporting goods store in Winnipeg. In addition to his hobbies (singing, photography, flying, motorboating, and golf) Gardiner ran hockey clinics in Winnipeg and always made himself available to charities for fundraising events. Sadly, a brain hemorrhage claimed his life on June 13, 1934, shortly after the Blackhawks' first Stanley Cup victory.

During 316 regular season NHL games (including 42 shutouts), Gardiner allowed only 664 goals for a 2.02 GAA. In 21 playoff games (including five shutouts), he allowed only 35 goals for a 1.43 GAA. Gar-

Ready for golf. (Photo courtesy of the Chuck Gardiner family)

diner received the Vezina Trophy (NHL's top goalie) in 1932 and 1934 and made the All-Star team four times. He was a charter Hockey Hall of Fame inductee in 1945.

John Peter "Johnny" Gottselig

One of the Blackhawks' all-time greats, Johnny Gottselig was born in a small hamlet on the Black Sea, near Odessa, Russia. When he was two months old, his family moved to Canada. They settled in Regina, Saskatchewan, and became Canadian citizens.

A January 8, 1939, *Chicago Sunday Tribune* article by Edward Burns elaborated on Gottselig's early life and immigration to North America, explaining: "John Gottselig's father, Albert, of Baden, Germany, and his mother, a Weber from Bayern, Germany, 'took up land' in a German settlement near Odessa, called Klosterdorf. They tried to make a living out of a vineyard but later learned of a more promising frontier, in Regina, Sask. So two months after their son John was born, they left Russia and set sail for Canada. For more than 30 years the Gottselig home has been in Regina, where Johnny, like all the kids in Regina, grew up with a hocky [sic] stick in his hand. Johnny's mother lives in Regina, and he writes her regularly, in German. And in the summer time they live under one roof and converse in German only."

Gottselig played hockey at Regina High School but dreamed of becoming a major league baseball player. A successful pitcher, he helped lead the Regina Winners to a provincial championship. Gottselig played for the semi-pro Regina Balmorals and St. John's College in Edmonton, Alberta. However, his big-league aspirations were quaffed when an injury gave him a "dead arm."

While studying at St. John's, after which he planned to attend law school, Gottselig and other students were required by the Oblate Fathers to skate recreationally, sometimes in 30-below-zero temperatures, and he continued developing his hockey skills. These came in handy when Gottselig's father died shortly before his college graduation. At that time, he decided to pursue a pro hockey career to help support his family.

Gottselig's path to the pros was marked with recognition. He was

John Peter "Johnny" Gottselig

Birthplace:	Odessa, Russia
Born:	June 24, 1905
Died:	May 15, 1986
Position:	Left Wing
Weight:	158
Height:	5'11"
Chicago Blackhawks Stats	
Uniform #:	7, 14
Games Played:	589
Goals:	176
Assists:	195
Points:	371
Penalty Minutes:	203
Seasons:	1928–41, 1942–45
Team Captain:	1935–40
Scoring Leader (Goals):	1929–30 (21); 1930–31 (20); 1931–32 (13); 1934–35 (19); 1938–39 (16)
Scoring Leader (Assists):	1931–32 (15); 1938–39 (23)
Scoring Leader (Total Points):	1930–31 (32); 1931–32 (28); 1938–39 (39)
Career Awards & Honors	
All-Star (Second Team):	1938–39, 1945–46 (Coach)
Saskatchewan Hockey Hall of Fame:	2014
Saskatchewan Sports Hall of Fame:	2018

a standout junior hockey player with the Saskatchewan Junior Hockey League's (SJHL) Regina Pats from 1922–23 to 1925–26. In addition to helping the Pats win the Memorial Cup in 1924–25, he played one game for the Saskatchewan Senior Hockey League's (SSHL) Regina Victorias that season. Gottselig suited up for the Prairie Hockey League's (PrHL) Regina Capitals in 1926–27 and the AHA's Winnipeg Maroons the following season.

On May 14, 1928, the Blackhawks claimed Gottselig in the Inter-League Draft, a move that Chicagoans would appreciate for years to come. A fan favorite, he played 589 regular season games. In 1938–39, Gottselig scored 16 goals and recorded 23 assists for 39 points, placing him among the league's top scorers and resulting in All-Star (second team) honors. Because of his leadership abilities, Gottselig was the

Blackhawks' team captain from 1935–40. A career highlight occurred on January 9, 1936, when he scored all four goals in a 4-1 Chicago victory over the New York Americans.

A 1930s *Chicago Stadium Review* profile described the "slim, keen-eyed, hawk-faced" forward as "one of the most honest and consistent players in the big loop, in addition to being one of the game's most tricky and brilliant stick-handlers." Not only was Gottselig an entertaining player, he had a knack for killing penalties. Elaborating on his capabilities as a penalty killer in the April 26, 1945, *Chicago Tribune*, sportswriter Charles Bartlett wrote: "The best solution to a Hawk penalty was to send John onto the ice. He became the deftest puck-nursing virtuoso in the league, tantalizing full-strength teams with his nimble touch in mid-ice."

Dick Irvin impacted Gottselig's formation into a talented NHL player by urging him to become a specialist at "ragging the puck" (keeping it away from the other team), a skill honed through hours of practice. "Gottselig took the advice seriously," wrote Jim Coleman in the December 7, 1950, *Lethbridge Herald*. "He practiced until his teammates thought he was daft. He wore a blindfold over his eyes and stick-handled until he was dizzy. A perfectionist, he could soon spin and pivot without looking at the puck and without losing control of it. Thanks to Irvin's advice, he was the last of the really good stick-handlers."

Gottselig acknowledged Irvin's influence in a March 23, 1946, article by John Carmichael, which appeared in the *Winnipeg Free Press*. "Dick taught me just about all I know about hockey," he said while coaching the Blackhawks in a game against Irvin's Montreal Canadiens.

In the same article, Irvin also recalled Gottselig's puck-ragging prowess, remembering a game played in Fort Erie, Ontario, between the Blackhawks and the Bruins. After Chicago drew a penalty, Gottselig's efforts neutralized Boston's power play. "Those old Bruins had size, weight, power," said Irvin. "Well, Johnny took the rubber on the face-off. Up and down center ice, between the blue lines, he wove a path of safety that sent the crowd into hysteria. For a full two minutes, not a Boston player touched that button and when, at last, the penalized Hawk returned to the ice, the crowd stood en masse and gave Johnny one of the most tremendous ovations ever heard."

Former Blackhawks player and manager Paul Thompson said Gottselig was not the type to hold grudges. "Several years ago Johnny was in his first real fuss with Art Somers of the Rangers," he wrote in the February 17, 1940, issue of *Liberty Magazine*. "It so happened that Somers had tripped the wing man, and Johnny did not like this business. Before one knew what had happened, the two were clawing at each other, and another rumpus was under way. When the game ended Johnny rushed over to Somers and grabbed his hand.

"'No hard feelings, old fellow,' he laughed. 'It's all in a night's work. And say, why not have dinner over at the house tomorrow?' The two dined together, and the following week, in another New York-Chicago game, they began the evening by taking a swing apiece at each other's head."

During World War II, Gottselig spent part of the 1940–41 season and all of 1941–42 playing for the Kansas City Americans, the Blackhawks' AHA affiliate. He also was involved with the All-American Girls Professional Baseball League (AAGPBL) from 1943–52. Gottselig already had experience managing the Regina-Moose Jaw Royals girls softball team in 1939. He piloted the Saskatchewan team to an international tournament in Chicago, where they were defeated. His familiarity with Canadian softball players likely was a contributing factor when Philip K. Wrigley chose him to manage AAGPBL teams.

In 1943, Gottselig managed Wisconsin's Racine Belles to the league's first championship, where they defeated the Kenosha Comets. Following the victory, the ecstatic players tossed their second baseman, Sophie Kurys, into the shower with her uniform on. Amidst the chaos, Gottselig shared his feelings with a reporter from the *Racine Journal-Times*.

In the paper's September 7, 1943, issue, he said: "Did you ever see such a series? I don't know of any ball club that ever rose to such great heights as this team. They said they would win in three games and they did, but who would have believed it possible. They're a great bunch of ball players and they played great ball. We played according to the book. Fans sometimes didn't agree with our strategy and I heard the wolves howl often but we did the best we could. In this series in particular, we played according to the book and in all three games the girls missed but one signal."

Johnny Gottselig demonstrates Chicago Stadium's new timepiece in 1943. (ST-17500 142-E1, Chicago Sun-Times/Chicago Daily News collection, Chicago History Museum)

Gottselig's popularity following the 1943 season was evident when some of the Belles attended games to watch their manager play pro hockey in 1943–44. Centerfielder Claire Schillace attended at least one game at Chicago Stadium, while third baseman Madelyn English saw him play at Boston Garden, where she was accompanied by members of the rival Rockford Peaches, including pitcher Mary Pratt and catcher Dorothy Green. Gottselig returned to Racine the following year and later managed in Peoria (1946–47), Kenosha (1949–51), and Grand Rapids (1952). Beyond managing, Gottselig also was an AAGPBL scout.

A National Baseball Hall of Fame article by Matt Rothenberg explained that, according to Jim Sargent's *We Were the All-American Girls: Interviews with Players of the AAGPBL, 1943–1954*, some former players were critical of Gottselig's management style and capabilities. Among them was Kurys, who claimed his softball knowledge was thin, and that he "didn't know that much about talent either." However, some sources credit Gottselig for discovering a few of the league's greatest players, including Kurys and underhand pitching superstar Connie Wisniewski.

After playing hockey, Gottselig was named the Blackhawks' coach in 1944. He became an American citizen the following year and eventually transitioned to public relations, assisting Joseph Farrell. Gottselig became public relations director in 1953 and held the post until 1962. He also did commentary and play-by-play work, becoming both the voice of Sunday night games on WCFL and providing hockey highlights on a Tuesday night television program. Gottselig later ran an instructional hockey school for kids at Ed Planert's Glen Ellyn ice arena.

Away from the ice, Gottselig was a skilled bowler who also enjoyed fishing, target shooting, skeet shooting, and motion picture photography. He also loved dogs. Burns's article featured Gottselig walking two Russian wolfhounds at the Glenwild kennels in Morton Grove, Illinois, including a world champion named Borisovitch.

Gottselig and his wife, Mae, once managed hundreds of acres of Canadian wheatland in Regina. However, they eventually made Chicago their permanent home, living on the city's Near North Side. Still working at age 80, Gottselig suffered a fatal heart attack at Chicago-Elmhurst Stone Co. on May 15, 1986, where he had been a sales representative for 24 years.

Harold C. "Mush" March

Harold "Mush" March left his father's farm to play for the City and District Junior Hockey Leagues' (City Jr.) Regina Falcons in 1925, where he remained for two seasons. When the Falcons combined with the Regina Pats in 1927–28, forming the SJHL's Regina Monarchs, March helped them win the 1928 Memorial Cup. Recognized as one of Regina's most outstanding athletes that year, he made the jump from junior hockey to the NHL when this was uncommon. After being discovered at age 20 by Dick Irvin, the Blackhawks signed March to a contract.

In the February 19, 1953, *Chicago Tribune*, sportswriter Charles Bartlett recalled the story of how the Blackhawks sent Bill Tobin to Saskatchewan to see the young Monarchs player Irvin had been talking about.

Harold C. "Mush" March

Birthplace:	Silton, Saskatchewan
Born:	October 18, 1908
Died:	January 9, 2002
Position:	Right Wing
Weight:	154
Height:	5'5"
Chicago Blackhawks Stats	
Uniform #:	5
Games Played:	759
Goals:	153
Assists:	230
Points:	383
Penalty Minutes:	540
Seasons:	1928–45
Career Awards & Honors	
Saskatchewan Sports Hall of Fame:	1988

Because March was under 21, his father, then working as a school custodian, handled negotiations in Tobin's hotel room.

"Tobin recalls that the entire conversation was between himself and March Sr. Mush sat in the corner, utterly speechless," Bartlett wrote. "Tobin told bright tales of life in the big leagues. Still nary a word from Mush. Bill then retired to an anteroom, where he stuffed $500 in one dollar bills into his handkerchief pocket. As he returned to March and his dad, he yanked out the kerchief, spilling the multitude of bills onto the floor. March had never seen so much money in his life.

"His father followed thru with the remark, 'Opportunity knocks but once, Harold!', and Mush finally agreed to let his father sign the contract for him. On Dec. 6, 1928, Mush made his debut as a Black Hawk against Ottawa. He went on from there to become a Stanley Cup hero, a golf professional, and a man whose ability and integrity as a league official merit respect everywhere."

Because of his small size (5'5", 154 pounds), in Regina March was given the nickname "Mush Mouth" after a character in the "Moon Mullins" comic strip. John Robertson, a longtime Chicago Blackhawks em-

Harold "Mush" March. (Photo courtesy of the Art Wiebe family)

ployee, once said: "Mush was a great player. He had a terrific shot and he had a thing of putting his stick over his shoulder and spinning around after shooting, catching the [opposing] players beneath the chin. He had a knack of doing that real well. He was a great scorer."

Although March was a forward, the Blackhawks benefited from his defensive backchecking. "It was a different program than it is now," said former off-ice official Jack Fitzsimmons in 1995. "He was a two-way performer; his offensive skills were always productive, and at the same time he was a defensive hockey player. He had many, many skills. You can't compare the game from the thirties and forties to the game today; it was different. But he was a credit to the sport and in fact, a credit to the sports world."

A profile of March in *30 Memorable Games Played by Chicago's Black Hawks* called him a "veritable speed demon" who backed down from no one, despite his small size: "Dour of face and almost expressionless, he played all the angles and used all the knavery known to the game in his desire to be the 'top man.' For a little guy, he was as saucy as a black fly, respected by all opponents and feared by all goalies."

March was the first player to score a goal in Toronto's Maple Leaf Gardens on November 12, 1931. When the final game was played in the arena on February 12, 1999, March and former Maple Leafs opponent Red Horner participated in a ceremonial puck drop. Making the occasion special was the fact that March used the actual "first goal" puck from 1931, a keepsake that was still in his possession.

After his playing days were over, March became one of the most respected linesmen in the NHL. He died in Elmhurst, Illinois, on January 9, 2002, at age 93. The year before his death, he dropped the puck for the 2000–01 season opener at United Center.

Donald Phillip "Donnie" McFadyen

Donald McFadyen's path to the NHL began in a very traditional way. In 1926, he helped the Calgary Canadians win junior hockey's coveted Memorial Cup, playing alongside future Blackhawks teammate Paul Thompson. However, instead of signing with a minor league club like most players of his era, McFadyen pursued an unconventional route, becoming a college hockey star in Milwaukee, Wisconsin, at Marquette University, where he received a full athletic scholarship. As team captain from 1928–30, McFadyen led the Marquette University Warriors to intercollegiate championships in 1928, 1929, and 1930, and was a two-time All-American.

At Marquette, a priest once surprised McFadyen by summoning

Donald Phillip "Donnie" McFadyen

Birthplace:	Grossfield, Alberta
Born:	March 24, 1907
Died:	May 26, 1990
Position:	Center, Left Wing
Weight:	163
Height:	5'9"
Chicago Blackhawks Stats	
Uniform #:	15
Games Played:	164
Goals:	12
Assists:	33
Points:	45
Penalty Minutes:	77
Seasons:	1932–36
Career Awards & Honors	
Marquette University Intercollegiate Athletic Hall of Fame	1972

him for an interview. "Grandpa, being of Scottish heritage, was Presbyterian," his granddaughter, Marya Callahan, explained. "He apparently thought he had screwed up really bad by being called in by a priest, who really just wanted to know if there were any other boys back home that played as well as he did. Apparently, the story is that grandpa said no; the only other person who played as well as he did, who could come close, was his brother, Harold." The interview apparently benefited Harold, who attended Marquette and was captain of its hockey team in 1931–32.

After earning an undergraduate philosophy degree, McFadyen broke into pro hockey with the AHA's Chicago Shamrocks in 1930–31, signing as a free agent on June 24, 1930, and remaining with the team for two seasons. "The Blackhawks offered me $3,000 but the Shamrocks offered $4,000, so I decided to go with them," he said in the May 9, 1986, *Toronto Globe and Mail*. On September 2, 1932, the Shamrocks

(opposite) McFadyen poses for a publicity photograph in 1929–30. (Department of Special Collections and University Archives, Raynor Memorial Libraries, Marquette University)

DONNIE McFADYEN
ALL AMERICAN CENTER
1929 & 1930
CAPT. 1930

McFadyen (left) and teammate Art Coulter (right) in November 1933. (SDN-075474, Chicago Sun-Times/Chicago Daily News collection, Chicago History Museum)

traded McFadyen to the Blackhawks for cash, and his pay was cut to $3,000.

During his four seasons with the Blackhawks, McFadyen was a steady player who was recognized for his leadership in the locker room. He also was versatile, contributing in penalty-killing and power-play situations. Chicagoans have McFadyen to thank for scoring two critical goals during the second round of the 1933–34 Stanley Cup playoffs. His contributions enabled the Blackhawks to defeat the Montreal Maroons and advance to the finals against the Detroit Red Wings.

While working as a sports reporter during the early part of his career, advertising executive Bill Marsteller was tasked with covering McFadyen and the two became friends. Callahan remembers her grandfather saying, "Everywhere I went, Bill Marsteller was writing about me, asking what I was doing on the train, at practice, and everything else."

After he made the pros, McFadyen's career path remained unconventional. While playing pro hockey, he managed to attend law school

McFadyen poses with a former Blackhawks teammate (unidentifiable) at his family's Arkansas fishing resort in 1982. (Photo courtesy of the Don McFadyen family)

at the University of Chicago, taking a semester's worth of courses each year and earning a Doctor of Laws degree in December 1933. After tasting Stanley Cup victory with the Blackhawks in 1934, he hung up the skates in 1936 to pursue a law career full-time. However, he remained connected to the game by working as an NHL linesman for four years.

"When I got my degree and got through a cram course for the bar exam, they wouldn't let me take it because I was not an American citizen," he said in a letter to Callahan. "So I had to get special permission and had to write the bar in Chicago. On a hot July day I passed. I got admitted the next year when I got my citizen's papers. . . . McFadyens are known for their Scotch adherence. Ever hear of Scotch tape?"

During World War II, McFadyen joined the U.S. Navy. He was aboard the destroyer USS *Southerland*, which was the first American ship to arrive in Tokyo Bay following the Japanese surrender. As the ship's navigator, he was presented with the first U.S. flag flown over postwar Japan.

"Gramps was gregarious, fun loving, outgoing, and had a real strong personality," recalls Callahan, who says McFadyen's Navy experiences made him an entertaining companion many decades after the war. "When I was in my 20s, we'd go out drinking. He'd spontaneously start singing old Navy songs and crowds of young people would gather around the table, listening to him talk about hockey and World War II."

After the war, McFadyen resumed his Chicago law practice in 1946 and was the city's Republican candidate for 19th Ward Alderman the following year, losing to John J. Duffy. McFadyen eventually opened a second law office in Pompano Beach, Florida, in 1958. After managing two locations for four years, he left Illinois for good.

"You would be surprised how many hockey fans I had as clients," he told the *Toronto Globe and Mail* in 1986. "But I had been going to Florida for holidays for years, and I had saved $100,000, and finally, I said, 'To hell with this.'"

In Pompano, McFadyen became an associate municipal court judge in 1966, holding the position for about 10 years. In his obituary, his son, Donald C. McFadyen, described him as "a tough, police officer's judge." However, McFadyen also had a poetic side, which he revealed in a letter to Callahan.

"I didn't know that you are interested in poetry," he wrote. "Me, too. I have an old idea on a poem to be called 'Pause.'

As you travel down life's highway,
Pause to explore the by ways . . .
This is where you'll find the true ways,
Of your country, beauty and your soul,

Nature hides its secrets & its beauty,
To those who search and pause,
Finding them in quiet and contemplation . . ."

At age 79, McFadyen was still practicing some law. Sadly, he passed away four years later after succumbing to a long illness. His legacy and contributions to Chicago's first Stanley Cup have a special place in the team's history.

Elwin Nelson "Doc" Romnes

Elwin "Doc" Romnes, a baker's son, came from very humble beginnings. "He told me that he would curl up magazines to put on as shin guards, and they'd be out on the lakes of Minnesota for hours and hours," explained his daughter, Virginia Hansen.

Romnes, whose parents had emigrated from Norway to the United States, excelled as a youth player at White Bear Lake High School and St. Paul Vocational (Mechanics Arts High School) in Minnesota before advancing to the college level with St. Thomas University in St. Paul. He went pro with the AHA's St. Paul Saints in 1927–28 and was acquired by the Blackhawks on October 28, 1930, becoming one of Chicago's most popular players.

Teammate Lionel Conacher once claimed that Doc was one of the best centers he ever skated with. Throughout his 10-year NHL career, which also included brief stints with the New York Americans and Toronto Maple Leafs, Romnes registered only 42 penalty minutes and was the first Blackhawk to take home the Lady Byng trophy (gentlemanly player) in 1935–36.

Several different stories exist regarding the origins of Romnes's nickname, "Doc." *Chicago Tribune* sportswriter Edward Burns once said Romnes picked up the name after taking a pre-med class at St. Thomas. However, Hansen explains that her father acquired the nickname in high school, when he began carrying his hockey skates in a doctor's bag.

There were only two American players in the NHL when Romnes broke into the league, according to the Hockey Hall of Fame. Doc is recognized as the first Minnesota native to play in the NHL and have his name inscribed on the Stanley Cup. This status presented certain challenges at a time when the league consisted mostly of Canadian players. In a March 7, 1985, *Pioneer Press* article by Don Riley, Romnes recalled: "There were times when nobody on my own Chicago Blackhawk[s] team talked to me. . . . They treated me a little like I was a thief. They wondered what an American was doing invading their preserve.

A young Doc Romnes poses next to his very first car. (Photo courtesy of the Doc Romnes family)

Doc Romnes relaxes at his cabin in Ely, Minnesota. (Photo courtesy of the Doc Romnes family)

Elwin Nelson "Doc" Romnes

Birthplace:	White Bear Lake, Minnesota
Born:	January 1, 1909
Died:	July 21, 1984
Position:	Left Wing/Center
Weight:	156
Height:	5'11"
Chicago Blackhawks Stats	
Uniform #:	12, 17, 19
Games Played:	309
Goals:	61
Assists:	119
Points:	180
Penalty Minutes:	42
Seasons:	1930–39
Scoring Leader (Assists):	1935–36 (25); 1937–38 (with Paul Thompson) (22)
Career Awards & Honors	
Awards:	Lady Byng Memorial Trophy (1936)
U.S. Hockey Hall of Fame:	1973

Gosh, how I'd try to be a good teammate and set them up! That's why I became a good playmaker, setting those fellows up so that they'd talk to me. I eventually got accepted, but it wasn't easy."

Hansen recalls that her father became close friends with several of his teammates, including Art Coulter, Mush March, and Johnny Gottselig. "He was pretty quiet and reserved, but he could have a good time, too," she says. "He liked to laugh. He wasn't an angel all of the time, but he was a good gentleman. He had a strong faith and was a very good Christian person."

On December 8, 1938, Blackhawks President Bill Tobin announced that the team had traded Romnes to the Toronto Maple Leafs for forward Bill Thoms. The following day, *Chicago Tribune* sportswriter Edward Burns said Thoms was "more rugged than Romnes, recently a faster skater, and always a better back checker than Doc." Tobin notified coach Bill Stewart of the deal by phone, telling him to have the players trade their equipment with one another when the Blackhawks arrived in Toronto for a game on December 10. Burns said Stewart "was

Doc Romnes, Art Wiebe, Earl Seibert, and Mush March pose for a photo, possibly during training camp in Hibbing, Minnesota, in 1936. (Photo courtesy of Ty Dilello/ Manitoba Hockey Hall of Fame)

delighted with the addition of Thoms, though he hated to lose one of his favorite individuals on the team with the transfer of Romnes."

Although illness eventually ended his playing career, Romnes remained involved with hockey as a coach, impacting many young players. After serving as Michigan Tech's coach from 1941 to 1945 (though play was suspended in 1943–44 and 1944–45 because of World War II), Romnes was behind the Kansas City Pla-Mors' bench in 1945–46 when the team took home the United States Hockey League (USHL) championship and playoff title. Between 1947 and 1952, he coached varsity hockey at the University of Minnesota.

"Hockey was really his life, even when he came down with rheumatoid arthritis and was quite ill," Hansen says. "He couldn't play, but then he went into coaching, even though the cold rinks in those days were really bad for his rheumatoid arthritis. When we moved to Colorado, he helped with high school. He was just always trying to stay in the game."

Paul Ivan Thompson

Born in Langdon, Alberta, Paul Thompson moved with his family to Calgary when he was five years old. There, he helped the Calgary Canadians (City Jr.) win the Memorial Cup in 1926. Thompson went pro with the New York Rangers and was one of the team's original players. In a February 17, 1940, article he penned for *Liberty Magazine*, Thompson reflected on the moment, writing: "I was a nervy kid, not as large as others, but willing to mix with any one. And after mixing, I was indeed a funny sight. But I got off pretty easy. At least, much easier than others."

Brother of four-time Vezina trophy winner and former Chicago Blackhawks head scout Tiny Thompson, Paul came to Chicago in 1931 after spending five years in New York, where he helped the Rangers win their first Stanley Cup. Thompson repeated this feat twice more with the Blackhawks, taking part in both of their first two Stanley Cup wins. An incredible athlete, he led the team in individual scoring six times during the eight years he played in the Windy City.

"Paul Thompson was an excellent player," former Blackhawks forward Cully Dahlstrom recalled in 1993. "He was great around the net and at shooting the puck." During his 13-year NHL career, Thompson scored 153 goals and racked up 179 assists for a total of 332 points. He was the American Division scoring champion in 1937–38. After playing, Thompson served as the Blackhawks' coach for six seasons, from 1938–39 to 1944–45.

Thompson appeared in print advertisements for R.J. Reynolds Tobacco Co.'s Camel cigarettes, alongside the likes of North American bobsled champion Ray F. Stevens and champion skater Jack Shea. One advertisement shows Thompson having a cigarette in his Blackhawks uniform, with the statement: "Camel's 'energizing effect' is a great thing. When I come off the rink, dead tired, there's just one thing I want—a Camel!"

Despite his status as one of the Blackhawks' best players, Thompson was not without his critics on home ice. In its January 4, 1936, issue, *Collier's* described one rabid fan who frequently hassled Thompson at Chicago Stadium, explaining: "There was one loud-voiced gentleman several years ago who spent the season riding Paul Thompson of

Paul Ivan Thompson

Birthplace:	Langdon, Alberta
Born:	November 2, 1906
Died:	September 13, 1991
Position:	Left Wing
Weight:	180
Height:	5'11"
Chicago Blackhawks Stats	
Uniform #:	6
Games Played:	365
Goals:	118
Assists:	146
Points:	264
Penalty Minutes:	192
Seasons:	1931–39
Scoring Leader (Goals):	1932–33 (13); 1933–34 (20); 1935–36 (17); 1936–37 (17); 1937–38 (22)
Scoring Leader (Assists):	1932–33 (20); 1933–34 (16); 1934–35 (23); 1936–37 (18); 1937–38 (with Doc Romnes) (22)
Scoring Leader (Total Points):	1932–33 (33); 1933–34 (36); 1934–35 (39); 1935–36 (40); 1936–37 (35); 1937–38 (44)
Career Awards & Honors	
All-Star (First Team):	1937–38, 1939–40 (Coach)
All-Star (Second Team):	1935–36, 1941–42 (Coach)

the Black Hawks. He was so conspicuous and so marvelously equipped with lungs that the Chicago newspapers began referring to him as The Voice. One night Thompson went crazy and shot three goals. He came off the ice beaming. 'I guess that'll shut the guy up,' he said proudly. The next night when the team skated out, Thompson came modestly but confidently near the end of the line. 'Great God, Thompson,' howled the man from the gallery in extreme amazement. 'Are you here again?'"

The Blackhawks' 1933–34 roster also included other noteworthy players, like forward Thomas John "Tommy" Cook. In 1928–29, the season before the Blackhawks claimed him in the Intra-League Draft, Cook earned most valuable player honors in the AHA as a member of the Tulsa Oilers. He was a consistent contributor throughout most of his eight-season career in Chicago. In addition to hockey, Cook grew

Johnny Gottselig (left) and Paul Thompson (right) in 1933. (SDN-075476, Chicago Sun-Times/Chicago Daily News collection, Chicago History Museum)

up playing baseball in his native Fort William, Ontario. The summer after the Blackhawks' Stanley Cup victory, Cook made headlines in Blenheim, Ontario, by managing the city's intermediate A baseball team to the Kent League title. He died on October 2, 1961, at age 54.

Rosario "Rosie" Couture, a speedy forward who also went by the nickname "Lolo," scored five goals and recorded eight assists in 1933–34, ranking seventh on the team in scoring. A gifted stickhandler and back checker with defensive smarts, the St. Boniface, Manitoba, native scored Chicago's first goal in game two of the 1934 Stanley Cup finals and recorded an assist in game three. Couture, who was friends with Chuck Gardiner and Johnny Gottselig, avoided going to parties but was a movie buff who enjoyed seeing pictures on the big screen with Gottselig. The two "movie hounds" once lived in the same apartment building in East Garfield Park. After seven seasons, Lolo's career with Chicago ended after he broke his stick on the head of the Montreal Maroons'

Left to right: Goaltender Chuck Gardiner, Tommy Cook (leaping), and Doc Romnes pose for an action portrait on November 11, 1933, at Chicago Stadium. (Le Studio du Hockey/Hockey Hall of Fame)

This unusual photo from Rosario Couture's scrapbook shows (left to right) Johnny Gottselig, Couture, Chuck Gardiner, and possibly Frank Selke in Chicago. (Photo courtesy of Ty Dilello/Manitoba Hockey Hall of Fame)

Dave Trottier in 1934–35. Couture was inducted into the Manitoba Hockey Hall of Fame posthumously in 1987, the year after his death.

Other standouts included defenseman Roger "Broadway" Jenkins who, though raised in Canada, was the first Wisconsin-born player to make the NHL. Johnny "Jake" Sheppard, who once played alongside his brother Frank with the Detroit Cougars, was an aggressive forward who ended his NHL career with the Blackhawks. Louis Trudel was a defensive forward who contributed to Chicago's Stanley Cup wins in both 1934 and 1938.

To my Pal
At Frite
from Louis
Best of Luck

Wright
Studio
21017

CHAPTER 4

Chasing Silver

As autumn leaves began to fall, Tommy Gorman arrived in Chicago on October 10, 1933. The Blackhawks' head coach held a conference with Frederic McLaughlin and manager Bill Tobin to discuss the upcoming season. McLaughlin undoubtedly appreciated his new pilot's sharp focus and determination.

"Gorman has no hobbies," a January 4, 1936, *Collier's* article explained. "He plays the worst game of golf in the Dominion of Canada, doesn't smoke, gets spiffed if he looks at a cocktail, [and] reads nothing but newspapers containing sporting scores."

Most of the team's players soon followed, arriving from Canada by car. After reporting to the team's offices in the Builders Building on October 14, they boarded a bus to the University of Illinois in Champaign, where preparations for three weeks of training camp were underway. Under the watchful eye of Athletic Association Business Manager C. E. Bowen, who played an important role in attracting the team to Champaign, the university narrowed its rink with wooden barriers to make it regulation size.

(opposite) Rookie Louis Trudel while playing for the St. Paul Greyhounds in 1933. (Photo courtesy of the Art Wiebe family)

Training Camp

The Blackhawks encountered fair weather and rising temperatures as they arrived in Champaign, but the atmosphere was undeniably electric as the university prepared for its homecoming football game against Wisconsin. Along with the Blackhawks, a large influx of football fans, alumni, and distinguished guests filled the streets of Champaign, including Illinois Governor Henry Horner. The night before, a massive crowd attended a pep rally, chanting "Beat Wisconsin!" against the backdrop of a massive bonfire and speakers like the Class of 1912's Otto Seiler, who had kicked a critical field goal in Illinois's very first homecoming game.

The Illini steamrolled Wisconsin 21-0, giving the university its first homecoming victory in four years. Following Illinois's third touchdown, the band played "Happy Days Are Here Again," the theme song of President Roosevelt's 1932 campaign. During a halftime interview, Governor Horner shared his excitement about the game and reflected on the Great Depression's impact on hundreds of thousands of Illinoisans. "Likening the depression to the enemy in a football game, he said that the spirit of the whole state was coming back, and that, at last, there was a definite will to pull up from the throes of economic stress," wrote columnist J. Benjamin Lieberman in the October 15, 1933, *Daily Illini*.

The Blackhawks began training at 1 p.m. on Sunday, October 15, with a 20-minute skating drill that was open to the public. Coach Gorman departed from a previous workout routine that began with a calisthenics program and told his team that they would do most of their conditioning on skates. The coach was pleased with the overall condition of his players. As they vied for a spot on the team, rookie hopefuls Tom Coulter, Bill Kendall, Jack Leswick, and Louis Trudel put pressure on returning veterans like defensemen Clarence "Taffy" Abel and Art Coulter (Tom Coulter's brother), and forwards Tom Cook, Rosario "Rosie" Couture, Johnny Gottselig, Roger Jenkins, Harold "Mush" March, Don McFadyen, Elwin "Doc" Romnes, and Paul Thompson.

During training camp, Gorman shifted Roger Jenkins from right wing to defense and was pleased with the results as Abel, Conacher, Art Coulter, and Jenkins gave the Blackhawks what some considered to be one of the NHL's toughest defense rosters. On October 20 Gorman gave

Leswick and Kendall the good news that they had made the club. The coach was so happy with the team's performance that he canceled their afternoon practice.

Lionel Conacher, another newcomer, had been the subject of hold-out rumors when he had yet to report for training by October 21. However, the star defenseman had been playing professional football in Canada, forcing him to miss a portion of the Blackhawks' camp. Also absent from camp was NHL veteran Tom Cook, who was recovering from an automobile accident in Canada.

On October 24, Frederic McLaughlin made the trek from Chicago to watch the Blackhawks train in Champaign. The previous year, the team held its training camp in Duluth, Minnesota. Although McLaughlin did not make the trip that year, the Blackhawks' publicity director, Joseph Farrell, had led the team's caravan astray, causing them to become lost in Minnesota's Northwoods.

Calling Farrell the "Hawks' erratic trail finder" in the October 25, 1933, *Chicago Daily Tribune*, reporter Edward Burns quipped: "The hazards of the trip caused most of the riders to lose confidence in automobiles in general and predict the return of the horse. Farrell sought to buoy up the spirits of the training camp travelers by constantly exhorting them to 'remember the covered wagon mothers,' and the great fortitude they showed in withstanding the hardships of homesteading the great West."

In Burns's column, McLaughlin added: "The widest concrete highway in Illinois forms most of the route to Champaign. I do not see how Farrell possibly could persuade my chauffeur to try a short cut over hill and vale via clay and sand trail and pontoon bridge." Despite challenges navigating the team across Minnesota, Farrell's lifetime accomplishments included climbing the pyramids of Egypt.

In Champaign, the Blackhawks enjoyed occasional sightseeing trips throughout central Illinois between practice sessions. On one afternoon trip, Farrell, perhaps working hard to keep the players amused, told them a tall tale. "Farrell, spying a sway-backed plow horse grazing in a pasture, ordered the automobile stopped," recalled sportswriter Arch Ward in the November 8, 1954, *Chicago Tribune*. "'Gentlemen,' said Farrell in a commanding voice generally used to cow ticket moochers, 'you are at one of the shrines of America. Yonder is Man o' War, the greatest race horse of all time. Thousands visit Big Red each year.' A skeptical Hawk observed that there were no other humans, besides the hockey party, within miles. 'Must be an off day for the tourists,' explained Farrell. The athletes were so convinced that all insisted on being photographed with Man o' War. . . . The pictures were sent back to friends in Canada, some of whom were smart enough to advise the victims that they most certainly had not been modeling with a race horse."

The Blackhawks treated Champaign residents and University of Illinois students to a series of four intra-squad games throughout their training camp. Coach Gorman organized the team into Eastern and Western squads. In the basement of University Hall, the Athletic Association sold two levels of reserved tickets, priced at 55 cents and $1.10.

Summarizing the third exhibition game on November 3 in the following day's *Daily Illini*, Marv Cohn described a team that seemed hungry for regular season play. "Bordering on the sensational, the Chicago Blackhawks last night sped through 60 minutes of ice hockey that thrilled 1,000 fans to the marrow and left them standing on their feet," he wrote. "In the peak of physical condition, the athletes scurried through the game, body checking, with sticks flying, taking daring chances which often finished with a resounding smash against the boards, and ever fighting for each possible break."

As the team entered the home stretch of training camp, a heat wave made its way across the Midwest. Scrimmages were impacted as Gorman had to stop practices periodically to clear dense fog from the ice. The team played its final exhibition game on November 4 before a capacity crowd.

On November 5, the Blackhawks capped off 23 days of training, during which the players skated an average of 2.5 hours per day. In addition to ice time, Gorman subjected the team to running, road drills, and even a few games of baseball. Following a quick morning drill, the players headed back to Chicago where workouts resumed at Chicago Stadium. "The squad is fit, and is ready to start their grueling 48 game season," claimed the November 5, 1933, *Daily Illini*. "Lionel Conacher, giant defenseman and Jack Leswick, American Association high scorer, appear to be the outstanding newcomers to the Blackhawk lineup."

Back in the Windy City, Gorman and most of the players took up residence at the Midwest Athletic Club (MAC)—a 13-story, L-shaped building at 6 N. Hamlin Avenue in West Garfield Park. According to a nomination form for the National Register of Historic Places, prepared in 1983 by freelance architectural historian Susan S. Benjamin, the club "could not have offered finer sports facilities—an Olympic pool, handball courts, a billiard room, a gymnasium with running track. This was in addition to a library, exercise and sleeping rooms, public and private dining rooms and two large ballrooms."

Not surprisingly, many players liked living at the MAC, which became a hotel after going into receivership in 1930. "It was a beautiful hotel," Art Coulter recalled in a 1989 interview with Antonia Chambers. "Some of the wives stayed in Chicago. Children mostly stayed in Canada." Former Blackhawks owner Arthur Wirtz acquired the MAC during the 1940s, providing training facilities for both hockey players and prizefighters.

In addition to the MAC, some players found other accommodations. At the beginning of the season, goaltender Chuck Gardiner and his wife, Myrtle, moved into the Hotel Cass, which offered a regular bedroom instead of the Murphy bed in the studio apartment where they had previously stayed. There, Gardiner's son, Bobby, played with the sons of teammates who also lived in the building, sometimes racing their tricycles down the hallway.

The Blackhawks were eager to start the regular season. Not only did the new combination of rookies and regulars have the desire to win, they also had chemistry on their side. "I'd like to think we were a pretty close team," Mush March once recalled. "We had some good players. We had Thompson, Romnes, myself, Lionel 'Big Train' Conacher on defense, and Charlie Gardiner in goal. All I can say is, we always had a pretty good club [during the 1930s]. Otherwise, we wouldn't have won the Stanley Cup a couple of times."

The 1933–34 Blackhawks also were "a tough team and a marvel on defense," according to the January 4, 1936, issue of *Collier's*. "One night in Montreal they bumped the Canadiens around with more than the usual ardor," the article explained. "When it was over, Howie Morenz, the great Canadiens forward, skated over to the Black Hawks bench. 'If

(above left) Left to Right: Roger Jenkins, Lionel Conacher, and Paul Thompson cook dinner in November 1933. (SDN-075731, Chicago Sun-Times/Chicago Daily News collection, Chicago History Museum). *(above right)* Charles and Myrtle Gardiner. (Photo courtesy of the Chuck Gardiner family).

---

there's any of you guys who hasn't hit me,' he said, 'you'd better hit me now because I'm just on my way home.'"

A Strong Start

The National Hockey League consisted of two divisions in 1933–34. The Chicago Blackhawks, Detroit Red Wings, New York Rangers, and Boston Bruins made up the American Division. The Canadian Division included the Toronto Maple Leafs, Montreal Canadiens, Montreal Maroons, New York Americans, and Ottawa Senators. These nine teams played a 48-game regular season.

In 1933–34, the NHL added an eight-by-five-foot "safe" area in front of each goal, designated with L-shaped brackets. The following season, this area evolved into an entire goal crease that was marked on the ice with solid lines instead of brackets. It also was in 1934–35 that 20-foot-diameter penalty shot circles appeared in front of each goal. Penalty shots, which had to be made from within the circle, were awarded when a player's shooting opportunity was hindered by tripping and the inability to pass the puck to a teammate.

The Blackhawks began the regular season on November 9, 1933. Among the 13,000 fans attending the season opener was owner Frederic McLaughlin, who watched the game from a box seat at the north end of the Stadium. He was accompanied by other members of the McLaughlin family and his wife, Irene, who wore a mink cape with a matching dress and beret. Many other members of Chicago society also attended.

A new NHL rule specified that no more than three players (including the goalie) of the defending team could stand in the defending zone before the attacking team carried the puck into that zone. The rule change, which carried a minor penalty for offenders, confused many of the Chicago fans, who witnessed a 2-2 overtime tie against the New York Americans. Chicago then faced off against Lester Patrick's New York Rangers, who had won the Stanley Cup the previous season.

The Rangers threatened their opponents with one of the most formidable lines in professional hockey. In addition to center Frank Boucher, a gifted playmaker, the line featured brothers Bill and Bun Cook, who played right wing and left wing, respectively. At the blue line, the Rangers had players like Ching Johnson, who was one of the game's hardest-checking defensemen, and the 200-pound Jean Pusie. Like the Blackhawks' Lionel Conacher, Pusie was one of the best all-around athletes in Canada, excelling at football, lacrosse, and wrestling. He was an effective two-way player, scoring a league-leading 52 points (30 goals and 22 assists) the previous season for the Western Canada Hockey League's (WCHL) Regina Capitals/Vancouver Maroons.

The Blackhawks showed more energy against the Rangers than they had against the Americans, outshooting them 23-7. Chicago won the rough, but well-officiated, game 1-0 thanks to a first-period goal by Rosie Couture, who joined Johnny Gottselig and Paul Thompson on Chicago's top line. After their first victory of the year, the Blackhawks left the following morning for Montreal to face off against the Canadiens for the season's initial away game.

In *Before the Echoes Fade*, Antonia Chambers wrote about the light mood as the team traveled by train to Montreal: "Donnie McFadyen and

Mush March played rummy; March's 'you big lucky so-and-so' when he lost could be heard the length of the car. But he was laughing when he said it, and as he pretended to lunge at McFadyen, those sitting nearby erupted into laughter. Johnny Gottselig sat across from Lolo Couture, smoking cigarettes and cracking jokes. Two seats ahead, Lionel Conacher contentedly puffed on his pipe and enjoyed the scenery. Taffy Abel and Doc Romnes absorbed themselves in a serious game of their beloved cribbage. Gardiner was engrossed in his usual game of checkers and after finishing off his opponent, turned to the hovering [sportswriter] John Carmichael. 'I don't always beat him,' laughed Gardiner, 'I'm not especially good at the game.' One of his teammates hollered, 'Here, here,' to the laughter of the group. 'I like it because it passes the time. It gives me something to do. And after all the principle in both games [checkers and hockey] is the same—trying to outguess the other fellow.'

"He then recounted a [checkers] game against Coach [Emil] Iverson the previous year on another long train journey. The game had reached a crucial stage, and had drawn a circle of onlookers. It was then Iverson's turn, and he was taking his time about it. The spectators grew impatient and urged Iverson to hurry it up. He made what he thought was a strong move, but Gardiner instantly countered, taking the last two kings of his coach and winning the game. Evidently Gardiner had a bit of a rough game the night before because a flustered Iverson blurted out, 'Why don't you do that in the nets?' Gardiner flashed back good-naturedly, 'I ain't playin against you in the nets.' The teammate-spectators all burst into laughter, in which Iverson joined."

As the Blackhawks faced off against the Canadiens, they encountered a team that, like the Rangers, had one of the league's toughest lines, featuring Howie Morenz, Aurel Joliat, and Johnny Gagnon. It was Gagnon who scored first. Mush March put the Blackhawks on the board with a late third-period goal, but Montreal won the contest 3-1 after scoring two goals while Lionel Conacher served a five-minute major penalty for a brawl with the Canadiens' George Mantha.

After their first loss of the season in Montreal, the team traveled to Ottawa to play the Senators. Under new coach and former Blackhawks

(continued on page 92)

RIDING THE RAILS

During the game's early years, train travel made playing professional hockey a different experience, in some cases forging stronger bonds among players. In a 1996 interview, former Detroit Red Wings and Boston Bruins defenseman Hubert George (Bill) Quackenbush, who was inducted into the Hockey Hall of Fame in 1976, recalled playing "eternal card games" while riding the rails. "We knew all the other players," he said, "a camaraderie that would be missed today."

Johnny Gottselig expressed a similar sentiment in an April 1979 *Hockey* article, explaining: "I think hockey players had more fun back then. We went out together between games and we made more personal appearances, not because it paid well, but because it was in our contracts. And, of course, those long train trips brought us closer together. Something interesting always happened on those train trips—like the time we lost a coach.

During the 1930s, the Chicago Blackhawks pose for a photo while traveling by train. (Photo courtesy of Ty Dilello/Manitoba Hockey Hall of Fame)

"One time while Iverson was still coach, we were coming back from New York on the train," he continued. "Emil was so anxious to read about our win that when the train stopped in Pittsburgh, he ran out in his pajamas and overcoat to buy a newspaper in the station. Before he could get back, the train pulled out. When we got to our next stop, there was a telegram waiting for us from Iverson. 'Send money,' it said. *We* said, 'The hell with it.'"

In the same article, Gottselig remembered another humorous incident that occurred on rails with his teammates, this time aboard a trolley. "We had a week off in Toronto one time," he explained. "One day after practice we got some beer and got on a streetcar to return to the hotel. As we rolled along, the motorman joined the party. In fact, he made an express run just for us, all the way back to the hotel. We went up to our rooms to continue the party, but about five minutes later the desk clerk calls to tell us that the streetcar was still stopped in front. The motorman had followed us up. He said he never really wanted to be a motorman anyway."

During this era, NHL teams traveled on several of the better railroads, which took great pride in dining cars that offered freshly prepared food. In a June 14, 1979, *San Diego Union* article, former Blackhawks forward Cully Dahlstrom said there was a pecking order when it came to the players' accommodations. "Usually we had a Pullman car of our own," he said. "Rookies got the upper berths and the better players or veterans got the lowers. I was assigned a lower berth midway [through] my first season with the Black Hawks and I had that assignment for the rest of my career."

Pullman cars typically featured 12 sections for passengers, a drawing room with its own bathroom and sofa, a smoking room and lavatory, and a separate lavatory for women. While rookies and sportswriters slept in upper berths on overnight trips, coaches and general managers usually occupied the drawing room. To give players optimal privacy, their Pullman car usually was at the front or rear of the train so that other passengers did not wander through.

Today, Chicago's O'Hare and Midway airports are gateways that offer virtually unlimited routes between the city and other destinations. A similar situation existed for rail travelers during the 1920s and 1930s. Chicago's "Big Six" downtown terminals (Union Station, North Western Terminal, Grand Central Station, LaSalle Street Station, Dearborn Station, and Central Station) "were the endpoints of almost all passengers arriving into the metropolitan region for more than 40 years," Joseph P. Schwieterman explained in *Terminal Town*, noting that in 1928 alone, hundreds of commuter trains and 440 intercity trains passed through these terminals.

The New York Central's (NYC) Water Level Route offered passage between the Big Apple, Chicago, and Detroit on trains like the 20th Century Limited, Lake Shore Limited, Wolverine, and Detroitier. The Pennsylvania Railroad also provided transportation between Chicago and New York on trains like the Broadway Limited, Pennsylvania Limited, and Manhattan Limited. The Broad-

Ready to travel in style, the Chicago Blackhawks wait at a train station, possibly in Canada, during the 1930s. (Photo courtesy of Ty Dilello/ Manitoba Hockey Hall of Fame)

way Limited and the 20th Century Limited were the premier trains on the Pennsylvania and NYC, respectively, offering the most luxurious accommodations. Some consider the 20th Century Limited to be the most famous train in the world. The Grand Trunk Western Railroad's Maple Leaf was one option for traveling between Chicago and Montreal. North of the border, players traveled on the Canadian Pacific and Canadian National railroads.

Passengers on the Pennsylvania Railroad traveled via Chicago's Union Station, while the NYC mostly used La Salle Street Station. Union Station was a grand facility with breathtaking architecture that operated around the clock. Approximately one city block wide and almost two miles long, it was a city within a city, offering such amenities as a barbershop, shoe repair shop, telegraph office, restaurants, and retail shops. Security was provided by a police force with its own two-cell jail. Those with medical needs had access to a dentist and a small hospital. A Men's Room and Women's Room, the latter featuring a nursery and beauty shop, provided facilities for showering and freshening up after long journeys. ∎

player George Boucher, the revitalized Ottawa club had realistic Stanley Cup aspirations. Although the Senators had won their first two games of the season, the Blackhawks defeated them 2-1.

Three nights later, Chicago faced off against Ottawa at home in one of the most brutal, fight-filled games at the Stadium in several years. In addition to a fist fight between Paul Thompson and Ottawa's Scotty Bowman, another brawl ensued between Chicago's Don McFadyen and Ottawa's Alex Shields. The Senators' Earl Roche cut Mush March over the eye, resulting in three stitches, although the incident did not draw a penalty. Thanks to first-period goals by Johnny Gottselig and Lionel Conacher, Chicago beat Ottawa 2-1.

After their victory over the Senators, the Blackhawks traveled to Boston to face the Bruins on November 21. The two teams had not met since March 14 of the previous season, when the Blackhawks forfeited after coach Gorman's ejection by referee Bill Stewart. Although the NHL investigated circumstances surrounding that controversial game and discussed it over the summer, the matter was ultimately dropped. However, it resulted in a new league rule giving referees the authority to award victories to non-offending teams when their opponents refused to play.

With Mush March sidelined by an eye injury and Tom Cook also on the injured list, the Blackhawks fell to the Bruins, who won 2-0 at the Garden. Gorman vowed the team would win their next match against Boston at the Stadium, with home ice advantage and the regulars back in the lineup, claiming that Cook had long been "poison" to the Bruins.

Following their physically punishing game in Boston, the Blackhawks were worse for wear. In *Before the Echoes Fade*, Antonia Chambers explained that, after traveling to New York for a game against the Americans on November 23, a 2-0 win, the team's hotel looked something like a hospital ward. "There was Art Coulter, reading a magazine, his upper lip mustached in white tape; Johnny Gottselig buying cigarettes, his right eye hidden under a diagonal bandage; Charlie Gardiner laughing off a white patch across his forehead; Paul Thompson's chin plastered with bleached gauze; and 'Mush' March with fresh dressing matting his right eye."

More than 16,000 fans, the largest crowd at Chicago Stadium in three years, came to see the Blackhawks shut out Boston on November 26. The game pitted Paul Thompson against his brother, Bruins' goalie Cecil "Tiny" Thompson, who eventually won four Vezina Trophies during his 12-year NHL career. It was Paul who assisted on a second-period goal by Johnny Gottselig that gave Chicago a 1-0 victory.

After beating the Bruins, coach Gorman put the now first-place Blackhawks through a strenuous workout at Chicago Stadium the following morning as they prepared for the season's first match against the Detroit Red Wings, who were led by the fiery Jack Adams. Memories of the previous season's encounters with Detroit were still fresh. The Blackhawks had beaten their Motor City rivals 3-1 during the first game of 1932–33 but lost every other matchup.

"Last season the Red Wings, looked upon as a group of remnants rescued by James Norris, of Chicago, at the outset were figured as a soft touch for the Hawks and insurance that the Chicagoans would get in the Stanley cup playoffs," wrote Edward Burns in the November 30, 1933, *Chicago Tribune*. "Now the Hawks are vastly improved, as indicated by the fact that they are leading the league and have lost only two games this season, both on the road. But the rub comes in the fact that the Red Wings also are better than ever." The high-scoring Red Wings now possessed the American Division's four leading scorers: Johnny Sorrell, Gordon Pettinger, Laurie Aurie, and Leighton "Happy" Emms.

Rather than traveling overnight and arriving on game day, Gorman and the Blackhawks left Chicago at noon on November 29 and were in Detroit for dinner. Gorman instructed his players to be in their hotel beds by 9 o'clock. Needing the extra rest was Art Coulter, who was suffering from a severe cold but decided to play anyway, defying the team's trainer and his physician. Despite their preparation and a goal by Lionel Conacher, Chicago fell to the Red Wings, who claimed a 2-1 victory on goals by Aurie and Emms, knocking the Blackhawks out of first place.

Heading into December, the Blackhawks had yet to face the lackluster Montreal Maroons or the Toronto Maple Leafs. After a 3-1 home ice victory over the Maroons on December 7, the team traveled to Toronto to play the Leafs on December 9, losing on a freak third period goal. A shot from Toronto's Charlie Conacher bounced off his brother, Lionel, and slipped past Chuck Gardiner, giving Toronto the game's only goal and a six-point lead in the Canadian Division.

In a 1989 interview with Antonia Chambers, Art Coulter recalled a situation involving Toronto Maple Leafs owner Conn Smythe. "One game in Toronto, he sat right in back of the net, yelling things at Gardiner, razzing him, trying to distract him, very unsportsmanlike," he said. "He would do any damn thing—insult opponents, embarrass his own players. Gardiner didn't say or do anything during the game. After the game, he chased Smythe around the inside of the rink, waving his stick in the air, telling him exactly what he thought. It was the funniest thing."

Having faced all their NHL opponents at least once, the Blackhawks rounded out the 1933 calendar year by winning or tying seven straight games. The streak began with a 4-0 shutout against the Red Wings on December 14. Three days later, Bill Kendall gave 14,000 Chicago fans a thrill by scoring three goals in a 4-1 victory over the Canadiens. Before this, Kendall had never scored a point in an NHL game.

On December 23, Chicago climbed to first place in the American Division with a 3-1 victory over the Bruins. Building on defensive prowess that was evident since the season began, the Blackhawks' scoring punch made them a consistent threat to all opponents. Especially dangerous on offense was the speedy pair of Paul Thompson and Johnny Gottselig, who made life complicated for opposing defensemen with their straight shooting and clever stickhandling.

After two consecutive wins on the road, the Blackhawks had played half of the season's away games by December 26. The team ended 1933 with a 2-2 tie at home against the Ottawa Senators on December 28 and began the New Year with four straight games on home ice. After suffering their first home loss of the season to the Toronto Maple Leafs on New Year's Day, the Blackhawks followed up with two overtime ties against the New York Rangers and Boston Bruins.

The January 11 matchup with Boston, which ended in a scoreless tie, was considered by some to be the most exciting game of the season to that point. The Bruins faced off against Chicago without star defenseman Eddie Shore, who was serving a 16-game suspension for injuring Toronto's Ace Bailey on December 12, 1933. (Frederic McLaughlin made an unsuccessful attempt to have Shore's suspension lifted before the game.) Bailey suffered a near-fatal cerebral hemorrhage from the career-ending injury. Following his recovery, the league held the very first NHL All-Star Game as a benefit for Bailey's family, and his jersey was the first in NHL history to be retired.

Making the game unusual was Boston manager Art Ross's decision to outfit the Bruins with light leather helmets for protection. Chicago fans disapproved of the headgear, claiming it made the players hard to distinguish. The decision also put Boston in an awkward position. In the January 12, 1934, *Chicago Daily Tribune*, Edward Burns said the Bruins "had to play tough hockey to convince the populace they hadn't become fraidy-cats. Hawk inquiries as to when they were going to sew lace on the hems of their panties did much to make the contest the spirited contest it was."

Referee Paul Rodden angered fans by disallowing a first-period goal Paul Thompson scored on his brother Tiny, claiming that Paul received the puck via an offside pass. The Stadium crowd became furious. When

Scene on the ice after the Ace Bailey/Eddie Shore incident, Boston Garden. (Photo courtesy of the Boston Public Library, Leslie Jones Collection)

All Star, "Stars" in the Ace Bailey Benefit Game 1934

BACK ROW LEFT TO RIGHT — THE LATE CHUCK GARDINER, RED BUTTON, EDDIE SHORE, ALLEN SHIELDS, BILL BRIAN, LIONEL CONACHER, CHING JOHNSON, NELS STEWART, FRANKIE FINNIGAN.

FRONT ROW LEFT TO RIGHT — NORRIE HIMES, LARRY AURIE, HOOLEY SMITH, ZIMMIE WARE, LESTER PATRICK, LEO DANDURAND, BILL COOK, HOWIE MORENZ. AURIE, JOLIAT, HERB LEWIS, MANGO, HOWIE MORENZ, JR.

C.C.M. SKATES — "CHAMPIONS EVERYWHERE"

(CCM Skates photo courtesy of the Chuck Gardiner family)

Boston's Eddie Shore, Babe Siebert, and Tiny Thompson in the Boston Garden locker room, March 1936. (Photo courtesy of the Boston Public Library, Leslie Jones Collection)

Rodden called a penalty on Chicago forward Jack Leswick in the second period, fans began pelting the referee with bags of peanuts and other items, causing a three-minute delay. During the same period, Roger Jenkins squared off with Boston's Joe Lamb in what Burns said "was better than the usual fight for it was waged while other players were following the puck to the opposite end of the rink, enabling the combatants to go to it without the customary interference. The battle ended when Jenkins sprawled his adversary with a neat clip on the chin."

Following a 4-0 win over the New York Americans on January 14, the Blackhawks traveled to Montreal to face the Maroons. When the train stopped near London, Ontario, some of the players, including Roger Jenkins, briefly joined a pickup game that was underway on a frozen pond by the tracks. Goaltender Chuck Gardiner watched the action from his window.

By January 1934, Gardiner was struggling with bouts of illness caused by chronic tonsillitis. After the Blackhawks lost to the Maroons in overtime on January 16, pain coursed through his body as the train took the team to New York to face the Rangers two days later. In *Before the Echoes Fade*, Antonia Chambers explained that the goaltender felt "pain shooting upward from his throat to his head, pain burning downward like liquid fire through his kidneys."

When Gorman asked Gardiner what was wrong, the goaltender simply said he had a headache. Although the coach gave him an aspirin, Gardiner endured a difficult night aboard the train, struggling to sleep. In the morning, his vision was clouded by black spots. Chambers noted that Gardiner had experienced a uremic convulsion, writing that "deep down he felt something was terribly wrong, something more than the tonsillitis which had plagued him the past two years, more than the chronic infection that he couldn't seem to shake off." As the season progressed, so did Gardiner's illness.

In New York, the Rangers beat the Blackhawks 5-0 in a match that was even more outrageous than the Bruins game several nights before. Chicago defenseman Lionel Conacher dropped the gloves twice. Late in the game he tangled with the Rangers' Doug Brennan in a fight that emptied both teams' benches. After being sent to the penalty box, Conacher began punching Brennan again (opposing players then shared the same penalty box). When Madison Square Garden spectators became involved, police were called to diffuse the situation and the players served the remainder of their penalties on separate benches.

After the tough loss to the Rangers, which knocked the Blackhawks out of a first place American Division tie, the team proceeded to go six straight games without a loss, ending the month of January with three consecutive wins against the Montreal Canadiens, the league-leading Toronto Maple Leafs, and the Ottawa Senators. The win over Ottawa put Chicago back in a tie with the Rangers for first in the American Division.

By early February, the Blackhawks seemed destined for the playoffs. Fans were enthused, and strong attendance had the club on track to at least break even financially, which it had done only once since 1926 (in 1930–31). Frederic McLaughlin credited coach Gorman and several tenacious veterans for the team's success to this point.

The Blackhawks and Maple Leafs fight for the puck on January 20, 1934, in Toronto. While that game ended in a tie, Chicago bested Toronto eight days later when the teams played in Chicago. (City of Toronto Archives)

In the February 3, 1934, *Chicago Daily Tribune*, McLaughlin told reporter Howard Barry: "From time to time, I bring a few of my friends into the locker room during the intermissions of the games. Their comments afterward are nearly always the same. They go into the locker room expecting to find a bunch of bored professionals planning to get through the rest of their night's work with a minimum of effort. Instead, they find a lively gang that has the spirit of a college team. Gorman gets the players in a fighting mood, and keeps them in it.

"We need a man like Conacher to exert a steadying influence on the team," he continued. "We had youth, enthusiasm, and speed [last season], but we lacked a cool, experienced fellow around whom the players could rally when the going got rough. The boys respect Conacher's judgment and they look to him when they're in a tough spot.

"I don't know of any man who throws himself into the game as Gardiner does," McLaughlin concluded. "He plays as hard in practice as he

Gardiner with son, Bobby, during the 1930–31 season. (Photo courtesy of the Chuck Gardiner family)

would in a Stanley Cup match. During an afternoon workout he'll drop full-length on the ice to stop the rush, taking a chance on getting the puck or a skate blade in his face."

During practices, Gardiner's wife, Myrtle, and Mush March's wife, Julia Byrd, often attended the team's practices together, and sometimes participated in skating activities with the men. Gardiner's young son, Bobby, also was hockey minded. By this time, he was playing midget hockey. Wearing a helmet that his father designed, the younger Gardiner aspired to be a goaltender like his father.

On February 4, the Blackhawks faced off at home against rival Bos-

McFadyen raises his stick in the air after scoring a goal, flanked by teammates Roger Jenkins (left) and Mush March (right). (SDN-075385, Chicago Sun-Times/ Chicago Daily News collection, Chicago History Museum)

ton. With tough guy Eddie Shore back in the lineup, fans packed the Stadium, but were disappointed when the Bruins won 2-1 in overtime. Following an overtime tie with the Red Wings four days later, the Blackhawks enjoyed a three-game winning streak, registering victories over the Canadiens, Senators, and Rangers.

Chicago fell into a slump on February 20 when the New York Americans beat them 3-1. During the next nine games the Blackhawks lost all but two contests (a 0-0 overtime tie with the Americans on February 22 and a 4-2 victory over the Maroons on March 4). The slump finally ended on March 13 when the Maroons pummeled the Blackhawks 6-2 in a fight-filled contest during which 22 penalties were called.

The Blackhawks suddenly came alive at the end of the regular season, winning two consecutive games against the powerful Toronto Maple Leafs on March 15 and March 18. Forward Don McFadyen put forth great effort to score a game-winning, third-period goal in the team's final regular-season contest. As Charles Bartlett wrote in the March 19,

1934, *Chicago Daily Tribune*: "The ruddy faced McFadyen, hardest working of the Hawks, was unbending himself to such an extent that his features began to assume a purplish hue. They beamed expansively when he finally slipped the puck past the nonchalant George Hainsworth."

The Blackhawks ended the regular season with a 20-17-11 (51 points) record, finishing second in the American Division and third best in the league overall, behind leader Toronto and second-place Detroit. The team carried positive momentum with them into the postseason, which began with a series against the Canadiens, who were second place in the Canadian Division, on March 22 in Montreal.

CHAPTER 5

That Toddlin' Title Town

n the quarterfinals, Chicago and Montreal played a two-game series in which total goals scored determined the winner. The team boarded the train for Montreal on March 19. Gorman was cautiously optimistic about the Blackhawks' prospects. Before departing, he shared his thoughts with the *Chicago Daily Tribune*, which appeared in the following day's issue.

"I think our chances of bringing the Stanley Cup to Chicago are bright," he said. "I think the series we are about to play will be the hardest of the three we are likely to participate in. All season it has been a nip and tuck affair between the Hawks and the Canadiens. We won three, they won two, the other finished a tie. We anticipate strong opposition, but if we can hold the Canadiens even or close in Montreal, the advantage will be with us on the Stadium ice next Sunday. The Hawks have the fighting spirit and that is what I figure will keep the team in the running right to the finals."

In the same article, Frederic McLaughlin offered his views on the postseason. "The 1934 playoff should be a thrilling race as there is little to choose between the six clubs," he said. "The Stanley Cup games are not likely to be a 'runaway' for any team. Two teams, the Blackhawks and the Canadiens, took the season's series from the high scoring Toronto Maple Leafs, and on the other hand, the Maple Leafs had the better of the American division leaders, the Detroit Red Wings, on the season's play. The Hawks will enter the playoffs in fine physical condition. I believe they are destined to go places this time."

Not only were the Blackhawks in good shape physically, they had the look of champions. Goaltender Chuck Gardiner had just won the Vezina trophy, beating out the Canadiens' Lorne Chabot. Gardiner also was named to the first All-Star team, along with teammate Lionel Conacher. In addition to Gardiner and Conacher, the Blackhawks were counting on defensemen Taffy Abel, Art Coulter, and Roger Jenkins to neutralize the powerful Montreal offense of Aurel Joliat, Wildor Larochelle, Johnny Gagnon, Howie Morenz, and Pit Lepine.

In the series' first game, Johnny Gottselig put Chicago on the scoreboard with a shorthanded goal early in the first period, but the Canadiens answered with two of their own. After receiving a pass from Doc Romnes, Lionel Conacher tied things up for Chicago during the middle of the second period. Gottselig contributed his second goal of the game during the last period, scoring easily on Chabot, who slipped and fell as Gottselig approached the goal. Coupled with Chicago's strong defensive play in the last 15 minutes of the game, Gottselig's goal gave the Blackhawks a 3-2 victory.

Following the opening game at the Forum, the series shifted back to Chicago Stadium, where the Blackhawks faced a strategic decision: play ultra-defensive hockey to protect their one-goal lead in the total-goal series or put forth an intense offensive effort. On March 25, a crowd of 17,600 assembled to cheer for the home team. During the first period, Montreal's Johnny Gagnon had the city on edge when he tied the series at three goals.

More exciting developments occurred during the opening period when Canadiens' star Howie Morenz collided with Mush March and left the game with a battered cheekbone and a broken right wrist. Tension mounted as the tightly officiated game progressed into overtime, with March scoring the series-winning goal after 10 minutes and 45 seconds of extra play, assisted by Paul Thompson and Doc Romnes. After eliminating the Canadiens, the Blackhawks headed back to Montreal to face the Maroons in the semifinals. Led by coach Eddie Gerard, their opponents had defeated the defending Stanley Cup champion New York Rangers in a two-game, total-goals series.

The Blackhawks arrived in Montreal on March 27, ready for more playoff hockey the following evening. Meanwhile, the Detroit Red Wings and Toronto Maple Leafs, both leaders in their respective divisions, were facing off in their own series. Except for Jack Leswick, who remained in Chicago with a leg injury, the entire Blackhawks organization made the trip to Montreal, including Frederic McLaughlin and spare goalie Joe Starke.

During the opening contest, Doc Romnes put Chicago on the scoreboard after only 43 seconds of play on a pass from Paul Thompson. Nearly 11,000 frustrated Montreal fans watched the two teams battle through a scoreless second period. Finally, Chicago came alive with two unanswered goals from Thomson and McFadyen early in the third period. The 3-0 shutout put the Blackhawks on solid footing as they headed back to Chicago for the second game of the series.

Arriving home on March 29, the Blackhawks practiced at the Stadium the following afternoon, and again on March 31. Apart from an injured Leroy Goldsworthy, who was replaced by Bill Kendall, the team was in good shape physically. As excitement mounted throughout the Windy City, WGN Radio's John Harrington prepared to broadcast the third period of the deciding game.

Although it seemed like victory in the total-goals series was in the bag, the Maroons had delivered upsetting performances before, including a 6-0 shutout against the Toronto Maple Leafs earlier in the season.

Blackhawks Publicity Director Joseph Farrell warned fans to cross their fingers. A crowd of 18,000, the largest of the season thus far, assembled at Chicago Stadium and saw the Blackhawks eliminate the Maroons with a 3-2 victory. Goals by Thompson, Cook, and McFadyen gave Chicago six goals for the series, to Montreal's two. Goaltender Chuck Gardiner was injured during the game and received five stitches over his right eye. For the first time since 1930–31, the Blackhawks had made it to the finals, where they faced Jack Adams's formidable Red Wings in a best-of-five series.

Jack Adams (right) and Toronto Maple Leafs owner Conn Smythe (left). (Walter P. Reuther Library, Archives of Labor and Urban Affairs, Wayne State University)

Jack Adams

During his 35-year run as general manager, "Jolly Jack" Adams built the Red Wings into champions. His team won the Stanley Cup seven times, along with 12 regular-season championships, seven of them consecutively. Loved, hated, honored, and respected, many different opinions exist regarding Adams. A symbol of both competitiveness and Detroit Red Wings hockey, he knew how to get results.

Adams joined the Red Wings, then the Detroit Cougars, as coach in 1927–28. The Great Depression was extremely difficult for the Red Wings. According to *If They Played Hockey in Heaven—The Jack Adams Story*, in 1931–32 Adams recalled how he had to chip in some of his own money to pay players. The Red Wings were spared from dissolution in 1933 when millionaire James Norris purchased the bankrupt team, which he renamed the Red Wings, and the Detroit Olympia. In 1934 Adams started to develop a farm system for the Red Wings that ultimately produced some of professional hockey's most legendary players, including Gordie Howe.

Larry Aurie (left) and Ebbie Goodfellow (center), pictured with teammate John Ross Roach.

The Kid Line

Detroit's roster included standout players like forwards Larry Aurie (right wing), Ebbie Goodfellow (center), and Herbie Lewis (left wing), who made up the famed Kid Line for the Red Wings during the 1930s. "They had a great team," recalled Mush March in 1996. "There's no doubt about that, or they wouldn't have been in the finals."

Aurie had been a key Detroit player since 1927, when Adams drafted the small, flashy forward from Sudbury, Ontario. After suiting up for the very first game ever played at the Detroit Olympia on November 22, 1927, Aurie electrified Red Wings fans during a career that spanned 11 seasons. He was an excellent penalty killer, known for his skill at ragging the puck, earning him the nickname "The Little Ragman."

Although he played an aggressive game, Aurie was cool under pressure. Adams considered him one of the greatest competitors he had ever seen, and many ranked him among the league's best two-way players. For this reason, the Red Wings relied on Aurie when they were shorthanded, and on the power play.

When Adams brought Ebbie Goodfellow to Detroit in 1929–30, he responded by leading the club in scoring. With the Red Wings, Goodfellow was one of the main attractions of his time, much like Gordie Howe was in later years. An unselfish playmaker, he possessed a hard, dangerous shot. Although Goodfellow was a star player, he was more workman than showboat. The original center for Larry Aurie and Herbie Lewis, Goodfellow was later replaced in the middle by Marty Barry when Adams moved him to right defense. He was inducted into the Hockey Hall of Fame in 1963.

Herbie Lewis spent his entire 11-season NHL career at left wing with Detroit, where he was extremely popular. When Adams brought Lewis to the Motor City in 1928, he made a move few could argue against. Over the course of his career, Lewis was "Ace of the Wings." He ranked among the NHL's leading scorers on a regular basis and was one of the league's best defensive forwards. A fast skater, accurate playmaker, and great sportsman, Lewis was inducted into the Hockey Hall of Fame in 1989.

Stanley Cup Finals

John DeVaney and Burt Goldblatt's book *The Stanley Cup* includes the following quote from former Detroit Red Wings goalie Wilf Cude: "I was having my afternoon steak before a game. I poured a hell of a lot of ketchup on it. I'd just started to eat when my wife Beulah made some casual remark. For no good reason, I picked up my steak and threw it at her. She ducked and the steak hit the wall. The ketchup splattered and the steak hung there on the wall. Slowly it began to peel, and I stared at it. Between the time that steak hit the wall and then hit the floor, I decided I'd been a touchy goalkeeper long enough. By the time it landed, I'd retired." The 1934 Stanley Cup finals probably contributed to Cude's touchiness.

The first game of the series was held in Detroit on April 3. The 15,000 fans in attendance included about 200 who traveled from the Windy City to support the Blackhawks. Like Chicago Stadium, the Detroit Olympia was lively and loud. "It was built for hockey," former Red Wings forward Carl Liscombe once recalled. "The first balcony was above the second-row seats from the ice. The people were only up in the air 40 or 50 feet, maybe. They were like sitting on your bench because

Coach Tommy Gorman and Chuck Gardiner, still bandaged up from Chicago's series against the Montreal Maroons, at the Detroit Olympia on April 3, 1934. (Le Studio du Hockey/Hockey Hall of Fame)

they could lean over the boards and yell at us. All the fans were rowdy back then. . . . I knew damned well when we played Chicago, we were going to have a tough hockey game."

Lionel Conacher scored the first goal for the Blackhawks at 17:50 of the first period, giving Chicago the lead. The game progressed through a scoreless second period, but Detroit tied the game with a goal from team captain Herbie Lewis late in the third. During that period, Detroit's Cooney Weiland sustained his third career nose fracture after a collision along the boards with Mush March.

During a second overtime period, Paul Thompson finally settled matters, scoring after one minute and 10 seconds of play. After stealing the puck from Detroit defenseman and former Blackhawks' captain Teddy Graham in front of the Red Wings' goal, Doc Romnes passed it to Thompson. As Charles Bartlett explained in the April 4, 1934, *Chicago Daily Tribune*, Wilf Cude "was still blinking when the red light went out."

The April 4, 1934, *Detroit Free Press* provided excerpts from the Red

From its opening in October 1927 until its closing in December 1979, Olympia Arena was Detroit's principal indoor arena for sporting events, including professional hockey. (Historic American Buildings Survey; Crane, C. H.; Massillon Bridge & Structural Company; retrieved from the Library of Congress)

Wings' locker room following Chicago's overtime victory. According to sportswriter Tod Rockwell, owner James Norris, Sr., mumbled that the Blackhawks "could do nothing but backcheck and wait for breaks," calling the team a "sort of backcheck, pokecheck and pray club."

Herbie Lewis yelled: "Hell, fellows, that's just a start! We've got their number now. It'll be a different story Thursday night." Calming his players, Jack Adams said, "Take it easy boys. Now mind what I tell you. All of us were a little too cautious tonight. We'll open up a little. We'll bump 'em a little harder."

Not only did Chicago's 2-1 victory give the team a strong start in the series, it was the first time the Blackhawks had defeated the Red Wings at home since February 1930, ending what some considered a jinx. During the finals, Gorman abstained from putting the players through any preliminary skating. Instead, the team enjoyed a tour of the Ford Motor Company factory that was sponsored by the Red Wings' Doug Young and the Maroons' Stew Evans. Following the excursion, Chicago

Doc Romnes works on his skates in April 1934. (SDN-076141, Chicago Sun-Times/ Chicago Daily News collection, Chicago History Museum)

trainer Eddie Froelich tended to players with aches and pains while the rest of the team rested in preparation for game two at the Olympia.

Excitement over the Blackhawks' success continued to build back home. WGN Radio arranged to broadcast portions of game two via bulletins received from a direct rink-side wire at the Olympia. During the penalty-filled first period, Chicago's Lolo Couture scored first at 17:50, after intercepting a pass from Detroit defenseman Burr Williams that was intended for defenseman Walt Buswell. When Tom Cook fired a shot at Cude during the second period, Buswell dove in front of the puck and was hit in the head, opening a cut under his right eye that required two stitches. He was carried off the ice by a teammate and two Chicago players.

Detroit's Herbie Lewis ultimately tied the game by scoring on Gardiner at 9:58 of the second period. However, the Blackhawks came alive during the third period with an effort from the line of Doc Romnes, Paul Thompson, and Mush March. Romnes put Chicago back in the lead with a goal at 1:38.

Defenseman Art Coulter scored next for Chicago at 5:34 in an exciting play with Johnny Gottselig. As Charles Bartlett wrote in the April 6, 1934, *Chicago Daily Tribune*: "Gottselig sprinted up center ice, with Coulter following up the right side of the rink. The Hawk left wing calculated his pace so neatly that he hoodwinked Young and Graham just in time for a perfect pass to Coulter. Art completed the maneuver by eluding Young and running the puck past Cude." Gottselig scored again at 18:02, giving Chicago a 4-1 victory. The Blackhawks played so well that the team received applause from some of Detroit's loyal fans.

In an April 6, 1934, article he wrote for the *Windsor Star*, defenseman Lionel Conacher described game two as a checkerboard performance that was carefully orchestrated by Tommy Gorman. "It may sound funny to say that a hockey game can be mapped out beforehand," he wrote. "Yet the Black Hawks have proved the theory can be put to practical demonstration."

Elaborating further, Conacher said: "Fans who saw Thursday's game at Olympia may not have realized that we were forced to change our tactics somewhat from Tuesday. We anticipated a switch in the defensive system of the Red Wings. We figured they would attempt to battle us at our own game. They did that very thing. They sent their forwards in to meet our attack, just as we had done against them Tuesday. They sent two players rushing after the play, with the third forward trailing behind. Our answer was to have the puck carrier either start up the side boards or shoot the puck up the side of the rink and allow our forwards to chase after it."

Looking ahead to game three, Conacher was cautious about making predictions. "Despite two straight wins on Detroit ice, I hesitate to say the Stanley Cup belongs to the Black Hawks," he wrote. "The Red Wings are just in the same spot the Toronto Leafs were. They have been beaten twice in a row on their own ice. They are in a desperate mood. So were the Leafs. If the Red Wings get the first goal in Chicago Sunday night they are going to be mighty tough to stop. They've only scored five times. They walloped us 3-0 their last time in Chicago, and on that trip looked like world beaters."

As the series shifted back to Chicago, both teams traveled to the Windy City on Friday, April 6. James Norris ordered his entire roster of

19 players to make the trip, though only 15 would dress for the game. The Red Wings practiced at the Stadium on Saturday morning and the Blackhawks at noon. By this time tickets for the third game had been sold out for two days.

"Promoters are shedding wistful tears that the match can not be staged in Soldier's Field, because they say the entire immense outdoor scene of Army-Navy Football games and other spectacular contests could easily be filled with paying customers," claimed the April 7, 1934, *Ottawa Citizen*.

After two consecutive victories, the only thing standing in the way of the "miracle sextet," as some fans were calling the Blackhawks, and the Stanley Cup was a final contest. Excitement reached an all-time high throughout the Windy City. A record crowd of approximately 18,000 people packed the Stadium with hopes of witnessing the very first Stanley Cup win in Chicago history.

The Blackhawks got on the scoreboard after only 28 seconds with a goal from Paul Thompson, assisted by Mush March and Doc Romnes. Although his nose was broken during the second period, Detroit goaltender Wilf Cude played spectacularly. That same period, Detroit's Gordon Pettinger tied the game and a subsequent goal from Laurie Aurie gave the Red Wings the lead. Johnny Gottselig answered for Chicago, and both teams were tied at two, but Detroit pulled ahead following a goal from Doug Young with only eight minutes remaining in the third period.

At this point, friction apparently developed between teammates Chuck Gardiner and Johnny Gottselig. An article by Joe Carveth in the April 10, 1934, *Detroit Free Press* said that, immediately after Doug Young scored for Detroit, Gardiner "skated over to the Chicago bench and had words with Johnny Gottselig. It was first reported that Gardiner directed a few blows in Gottselig's direction, but Johnny denied today that he had been hit. This flareup, however, upset the Hawks' morale and they were a much different team, an unorganized band, over the remainder of the route."

Putting Gardiner's outburst into context, illness had affected his normally spectacular goaltending. Despite frequent visits to the hospital for a kidney condition, the remarkable netminder had never missed a game. In a state of exhaustion, he collapsed at one point. As his strength faded, things turned sour for the Blackhawks when Cooney Weiland scored a fourth Detroit goal, followed by a fifth from Laurie Aurie with only seven seconds left on the clock.

Carveth's article touted that, following their 5-2 win at the Stadium, Detroit was "bubbling confidence." In fact, the sportswriter claimed the Red Wings had cracked the Blackhawks' defensive code, writing: "The pestiferous back-checking in mid-ice that marked the Hawks' play in Detroit was nullified by fast breaking forwards who, instead of starting their plays back of the blue line, broke from mid-ice and were in full stride before the Hawks could catch them. They found a way to beat the Hawks' back-checking, and how well they did it is reflected in the score. Any team that beats Chuck Gardiner five times in 60 minutes is playing a lot of good hockey."

On April 10, the Blackhawks and Red Wings were both given a day of rest and relaxation before the next game. Many of the Detroit players spent part of their day watching the Chicago Cubs practice at Wrigley Field, though Lord Stanley's silver cup must have dominated all their thoughts. "Manager Adams is elated over the impressive victory of his team Sunday night," Carveth wrote. "The Wings' pilot now can see nothing but another victory Tuesday and the fifth and deciding game in Detroit Thursday night."

Following the tough loss, the Blackhawks sent Gardiner to Milwaukee for two days of rest. Johnny Gottselig once explained that in addition to his physical illness, worrying often sapped Gardiner's strength. Although management had doubts about his ability to continue playing, Chicago's formidable puck-stopper was in goal for the entire Stanley Cup final game on April 10, 1934.

That day, a primary election was held in Cook County. In its April 11, 1934, issue, the *Chicago Daily Tribune* described the election as "the most peaceful and orderly election in the history of the county," with "practically no violence and not one report of gunplay." Complying with a city ordinance and state law, no liquor was sold when polls opened, and saloonkeepers kept their doors closed.

With game night temperatures hovering around 69 degrees, fans packed into Chicago Stadium, full of pent-up energy. The influx congested traffic so badly that a cab ride from the Loop to the Stadium took 35 minutes. Many fans parked vehicles six blocks from the arena and walked the rest of the way.

As Chicago and Detroit faced off again, the game was not just a battle for the Stanley Cup; it symbolized a bitter rivalry between opposing owners Frederic McLaughlin and James Norris, Sr. "Norris and McLaughlin, wealthy residents of Lake Forest, Ill., mingle in the same society, but that doesn't prevent them from being keen rivals," Sports Editor M. F. Drukenbrod wrote in the January 26, 1934, *Detroit Free Press*. "Rather it adds to the rivalry, one that began some years back when they headed Chicago teams in different hockey leagues. This pair eagerly await every clash between their teams, members of the same division in the National Hockey League, and the one who wins never fails to gloat over his triumph. . . . Each will willingly spend thousands of dollars for players in his desire to have a team that will beat that of his Lake Forest neighbor."

Opening at a fast pace, the Blackhawks played careful hockey following their loss in the previous game. When Detroit's Gus Marker was sent to the penalty box for charging Gottselig, Gorman put forwards March, Thompson, Romnes, and Cook on the ice, leaving only defenseman Coulter to protect Gardiner. The quartet hammered Wilf Cude with a sustained barrage of shots for almost two minutes but was unable to score. The Blackhawks maintained this offensive pressure through the remainder of the period. Gottselig and McFadyen made an exciting rush with only three minutes left on the clock, but Cude sprawled in front of the goal to stop the shot.

Detroit was not without its chances during the opening period. Early on, Herbie Lewis nearly scored on Gardiner with a high shot. He almost succeeded on the rebound as well, but the puck was swept away in the nick of time by Chicago defenseman Roger Jenkins. After that, the Red Wings went at full steam in their attempt to score, only gaining an advantage for a short while. Although they had a power-play opportunity when Rosie Couture was penalized for tripping, Detroit failed to capitalize and the game's opening round ended with no score.

During the second period, Mush March electrified the Stadium crowd when he completely escaped Detroit's defense on a mad rush

Chuck Gardiner, Leroy Goldsworthy, Roger Jenkins, Doc Romnes, Taffy Abel, and Louis Trudel in 1934. (SDN-076145, Chicago Sun-Times/Chicago Daily News collection, Chicago History Museum)

for Cude, but his shot just barely missed the net. Tom Cook also nearly scored but was denied when Cude deflected his shot. Despite offensive pressure from Cook, Trudel, and Goldsworthy, the Blackhawks were unable to overcome the Red Wings' defense and the second period ended with no score.

During the third period the Blackhawks were driven by the desire to end the series and claim their very first Stanley Cup, while Detroit fought desperately to avoid elimination. Cook, Trudel, and Goldsworthy excited fans with some of the fastest skating of the game, creating a close but unsuccessful scoring opportunity for Cook. Detroit's Hap Emms gave Gardiner his toughest moment of the contest with a high, hard shot that caused the ill goalie to fall and take a time out to catch his breath. After three grueling periods, the scoreless game progressed into the first of two overtime periods.

Several near fights developed in overtime as the tension mounted, but no penalties were called. A window of opportunity opened about nine minutes into the second overtime round when Detroit's Ebbie Goodfellow was penalized for tripping Tom Cook. Gorman immediately sent Thompson, Romnes, Conacher, and March onto the ice for the power play. To this point, only two penalties had been called during the entire game, both during the opening period of regular play.

With Goodfellow in the penalty box, March received a pass from Romnes, who had maintained control of the puck despite a bump from Detroit's Teddy Graham. March then fired a historic shot that whizzed past Cude, securing the first Stanley Cup in Chicago history. "We had a faceoff in their [Detroit's] end," March recalled in 1996. "Romnes got the puck back to me and I just whacked it!"

After scoring the goal, which ended 90 minutes and five seconds of play, March skated over to Cude, patted him on the back sympathetically, and retrieved the historic puck from the left-hand corner of the net. "I think Cude was startled to see me diving in after it, but I just had to have it," March said in George Vass's book, *The Chicago Black Hawks Story*. "It was probably the biggest goal I ever scored."

Chicago players rushed Cude to congratulate the slim goaltender, who tried to rebuff their embraces. A jubilant Johnny Gottselig threw his stick into the air, striking an usher halfway down the ice. Most of the Detroit players made a quick exit, except for Cude, who was held back by throngs of Chicago players.

This photograph from Doc Romnes's scrapbook shows Mush March's historic goal in action. (Photo courtesy of the Doc Romnes family)

The Stanley Cup is presented to Major Frederic McLaughlin (center) as NHL President Frank Calder, coach Tommy Gorman (far right, holding hat), and players look on. (SDN-076069, Chicago Sun-Times/Chicago Daily News collection, Chicago History Museum)

Some 10 minutes after the historic goal, the Stadium crowd continued to cheer for the Blackhawks and Cude, who remained on the ice. In the April 11, 1934, *Detroit Free Press*, Jack Carveth wrote: "Miniature bombs were tossed on the ice as the mob shouted, 'We want March.' March stood with his mates long after the game was over, posing for photographers and hearing the plaudits of Hawk supporters." NHL President Frank Calder eventually presented the Blackhawks with the Stanley Cup at center ice, and March was escorted by teammate Louis Trudel for a victory lap around the rink.

In an *American Legion Monthly* article he wrote just before the start of the 1935–36 hockey season, Frederic McLaughlin recalled his reaction to the historic victory. "Nobody, I honestly believe, realized that a score had been made, the game and series ended, the Stanley Cup and championship pennant earned for Chicago, until March dived headlong into the net to retrieve the puck which had made the winning score," he explained. "Perhaps the goal judge's red light had already flashed on above the net to signal the Black Hawk point. I did not see it, nor did anyone else I have asked about it, until March went in after the rubber. Then, believe it or not, the entire crowd sat there for perhaps twenty minutes talking over the game, until finally somebody had gumption enough to start for home.

"Surprisingly enough, my first emotion was not jubilation that we had won," he continued. "Rather it was relief that the game was over, that the over-tired players could finally get off the ice. The feeling would have been identical had Detroit won instead of the Black Hawks. Nor does this mean that I am unduly sympathetic or soft-hearted. Probably every spectator in the huge crowd was suffering mentally along with those panting skaters as though he himself were one of them. It was the kind of game that gets under your skin, no matter how thick and tough your skin may be."

In that final game, Cude stopped 53 shots and Gardiner stopped 40. It was a twist of fate that Gardiner and Cude played goal on the opposing teams. As boys, they were friends in Winnipeg and walked back and forth to school together. Before removing his uniform, Detroit's Teddy Graham, who had spent the previous five seasons with Chicago, stopped by the Blackhawks' dressing room to congratulate his former teammates.

Graham encountered a darker atmosphere in Detroit's locker room. "Owner James Norris of the Wings took the defeat with a broad grin," Carveth wrote. "He lauded the work of his players just as he did after the Hawks took two straight from the Wings in Detroit. But the players did not take it so well. They plainly were broken-hearted at the turn of events."

Norris's grin likely masked feelings of anger and disappointment. More than three years later, his rivalry with McLaughlin remained intact. In its October 14, 1937, issue, the Detroit Free Press noted: "For years the Major and James Norris, the elder, have been enemies in private although when they meet in public they bow politely and formally. Thus it is that the Red Wing owner likes to get a snicker at the Major as well as does [manager Jack] Adams."

A celebration followed in the Stadium Grill, where a jubilant Mc-

Paul Thompson (left) and Tommy Gorman (right) celebrate Chicago's Stanley Cup victory over Detroit. (Walter P. Reuther Library, Archives of Labor and Urban Affairs, Wayne State University)

Laughlin hosted a party for players and reporters. True to his predictions at the beginning of the season, the Blackhawks were world champions. The official post-game party paled in comparison to the massive parades following Chicago's 21st century Stanley Cup victories. Several players had already left town the evening after the big victory, and most were soon traveling to their respective hometowns.

On April 11, the sports section of the *Detroit Free Press* featured a photo of a grinning Jack Adams, leaning on the boards from behind the bench, hands crossed. A caption from Adams read: "The boys did great work, and we will be back with a winner next year." Although Adams was wrong (the Montreal Maroons won the Stanley Cup in 1934–35), Detroit claimed the prize in both 1935–36 and 1936–37.

Roger "Broadway" Jenkins paid up on a bet he had made with Gardiner earlier in the season (that the team would not make the playoffs). On April 12, Jenkins wheeled Gardiner around a Chicago Loop block in

(continued on page 123)

CHICAGO'S FIRST HOCKEY CHAMPIONS

Although the Blackhawks brought the first Stanley Cup to Chicago in 1934, the Chicago Shamrocks gave the city its first national hockey championship. The Shamrocks defeated the Duluth Hornets to win the American Hockey League (AHL) title on April 8, 1932, with a 4-3 overtime victory. In goal for the Shamrocks was Mike Karakas, an American who later helped the Blackhawks win their second Stanley Cup in 1938.

The Great Depression, which arrived shortly after Chicago Stadium opened, facilitated the Shamrocks' formation. The arena's investors, including Paddy Harmon and James Norris, saw another professional hockey team as a revenue source during uncertain times. This ultimately brought a new AHL franchise to the Windy City and the Stadium.

Norris, who owned a controlling stake in the Stadium, had been unsuccessful in securing rights for a second NHL team in

Mike Karakas in goal for the Chicago Shamrocks. (Photo courtesy of HockeyGods.com)

Chicago. Instead, he bought the Shamrocks of the minor league American Hockey Association (AHA), which changed its name to the AHL to become a major league circuit. The new club was led by President Tom Shaughnessy, an attorney who had coached the Blackhawks in 1929–30. The Shamrocks were despised by NHL President Frank Calder, who dubbed the AHL an outlaw league.

The Shamrocks received preferential scheduling arrangements from Chicago Stadium's owners. This threw a wrench in the NHL's 1931–32 schedule when the Blackhawks could not play games there on Tuesday and Thursday nights. Adding fuel to the fire, the Shamrocks agreed to play the Blackhawks in a preseason charity game (a fundraiser for the unemployed), but Calder refused to allow it.

According to John Wong's book, *Lords of the Rinks*, which explored the situation in detail, Frederic McLaughlin viewed the Shamrocks as a threat to the Blackhawks' fan base. In a letter to Calder, he argued that Chicagoans, still relatively unfamiliar with hockey and the quality of different leagues, were preoccupied with league standings. If the Shamrocks dominated the AHL, McLaughlin worried about the resulting impact on his NHL club.

As one of the wealthiest grain operators in Chicago, and a former hockey player himself, Norris had both the funds and the passion to be a successful team owner. His controlling stake in the Stadium gave him the power to make things difficult by refusing to share the arena. A frustrated Norris had made several attempts to acquire the Blackhawks, only to be rebuffed by McLaughlin.

The AHL struggled financially and reverted to minor-league status after only two seasons, once again becoming the AHA. Norris ultimately dissolved the Shamrocks after learning that Detroit's NHL franchise was for sale. After acquiring the Detroit Falcons, Norris renamed the team the Red Wings, building the club into an NHL powerhouse with coach Jack Adams. Norris died in 1952. Two years later, his son, James Norris, Jr., became co-owner of the Chicago Blackhawks with Arthur Wirtz. ∎

Former Chicago Blackhawks teammates Lionel Conacher (left) of the Montreal Maroons and Roger Jenkins of the Boston Bruins serve a penalty in 1935–36 for being rough on the ice. (Photo courtesy of the Boston Public Library, Leslie Jones Collection)

a wheelbarrow, trailed by "judges" Lionel Conacher and Johnny Gottselig, who were present to ensure the bet was honored as promised. Conacher added his own humorous touch by making Gardiner carry three roses during the wheelbarrow ride. This was the closest thing to a parade the players experienced.

A Sad Ending

Chuck and Myrtle Gardiner arrived home in Winnipeg on April 20. Sadly, the celebrated goalie never returned to the Windy City. He died at age 29 in Winnipeg's St. Boniface Hospital on June 13, 1934, after collapsing at home and slipping into a coma. The uremic convulsions caused by his tonsil infection produced a fatal brain hemorrhage (Gardiner also suffered from kidney and stomach problems).

In the June 14, 1934, *Chicago Daily Tribune*, Blackhawks manager Bill Tobin explained that when he learned about Gardiner's illness, the team offered to send specialists to treat him. However, his condition had worsened quickly, and he was comatose for almost three days before passing away. "Gardiner was loved by everybody who knew him," said Tobin. "He was hockey's greatest goal tender. His loss is going to be a terrible handicap to the team."

In a 1989 interview with Antonia Chambers, Vince Leah, who worked as a reporter for the *Winnipeg Tribune*, recalled the Winnipeg community's reaction to Gardiner's death, commenting: "He had a lot of courage. Nobody knew he was ill. . . . He had

Chuck Gardiner. (Photo courtesy of the Chuck Gardiner family)

one of the biggest funerals in the history of the city. There was an overflow crowd at the church—about 1,000 people and over 2,000 outside. He was very pleasant, a very warm person. He didn't brush you off. He talked to everybody. You always saw him talking to people when he was coming down the street. If you went up to him with your autograph book he would always say 'sure' and sign it with a smile."

In 1995, longtime Hockey Hall of Fame volunteer Tom Gaston recalled a memorial service held at Maple Leaf Gardens for Gardiner. "At the north end, they had the net set up and special colored lights," he said. "They lowered a big cut-out of Charlie down from the rafters in front of the net, and they had flowers draped around it. I happened to be there that night when they paid tribute to Charlie. When a team in another city honors a man in this respect it shows that he's well-liked, well loved, and well respected."

Gardiner's death was not the only tragedy that befell the Blackhawks following their first Stanley Cup victory. In July 1934, 24-year-old rookie forward Jack "Newsy" Leswick arrived in Winnipeg to vacation

Onlookers pay tribute to Chuck Gardiner at a memorial service. (Photo courtesy of the Chuck Gardiner family)

with his brother, Pete, and two others. Leswick had been in town for several weeks when, on August 2, he disappeared from his apartment. Two days later his body was found in the muddy Assiniboine River near Winnipeg's River Park. Leswick's gold Stanley Cup watch and other personal items were missing, along with his Chevrolet Coach.

Police considered Leswick's death to be a suicide, but given the circumstances, Pete Leswick and others believed he had been murdered following a holdup. "The theory that young Leswick took his own life was rejected by his brother," said an article in the August 7, 1934, *Winnipeg Tribune*. "He was aggressive in character and suicide would be the furthest thing from his mind, his brother declared." Coroner Dr. C. H. Speechly, however, claimed Leswick's body contained no evidence of violence and attributed the death to drowning. "There was nothing to indicate murder," he said in the August 7, 1934, *Edmonton Journal*.

At the time of his death, Chicago had traded Leswick to the International-American Hockey League's (IAHL) Cleveland team in exchange for Norm Locking. Before it was returned to Saskatoon, Saskatchewan, where his mother lived, Leswick's body was identified by former Chicago teammates Leroy Goldsworthy and Rosie Couture, along with a trainer named Billy Hughes who had been associated with the Duluth Hornets during Leswick's time with that team. He left behind eight brothers and sisters.

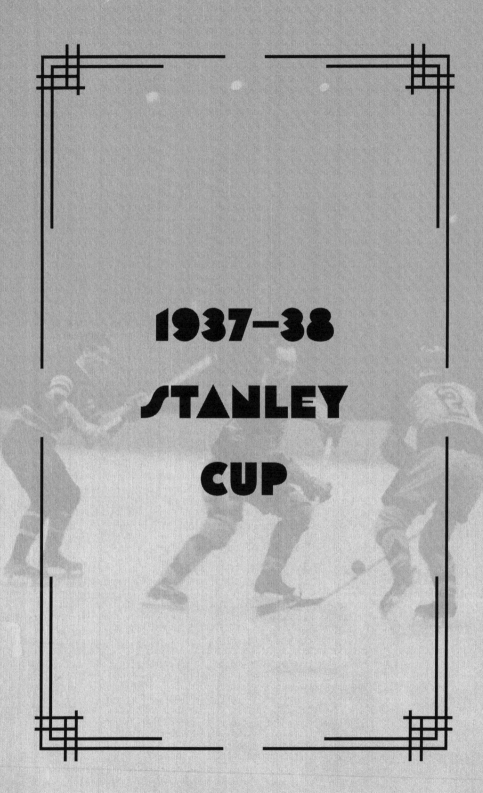

1937—38 STANLEY CUP

Under coach Clem Loughlin, the Blackhawks had made the playoffs in both 1934–35 and 1935–36, losing in the quarter-finals to the Montreal Maroons and the New York Americans, respectively. Finishing fourth (14-27-7) in the American division, the Blackhawks failed to make a postseason appearance in 1936–37. That season, an ankle injury sidelined Mush March for 12 games and a charley horse kept Doc Romnes off the ice for 22 games. This was a major blow; in 1935–36, the line of March, Romnes, and Paul Thompson led the league with 46 goals, 67 assists, and 113 points.

In March of 1937, Frederic McLaughlin announced that Loughlin would continue to manage the Blackhawks in 1937–38. However, after being involved with hockey for more than 20 years, Loughlin decided to retire in May so that he could run a hotel he owned in Viking, Alberta, and manage his wheat farm. McLaughlin praised Loughlin for his character and high ideals, expressed regret over his departure, and named his successor: professional baseball umpire and NHL referee Bill Stewart.

The Blackhawks pose for a photo on January 16, 1936.
(SDN-078530, Chicago Sun-Times/Chicago Daily News
collection, Chicago History Museum)

NO SMOKING

The Chicago Blackhawks pose for a photo with coach Clem Loughlin in 1934–35. (Photo courtesy of the Doc Romnes family)

Left to right: Art Coulter, Doc Romnes, Mike Karakas, Paul Thompson, [unidentified], and Don McFadyen in 1935–36. (Photo courtesy of Ty Dilello/Manitoba Hockey Hall of Fame)

1937-38 Chicago Blackhawks

Name	Position	Games	Goals	Assists	Points	Penalty Minutes
Glenn Brydson	RW	19	1	3	4	6
Marty Burke	D	12	0	0	0	8
Bert Connolly	LW	16	1	2	3	4
Cully Dahlstrom	C	48	10	9	19	11
Johnny Gottselig (C)	LW	48	13	19	32	22
Oscar Hanson	C	8	0	0	0	0
Vic Heyliger	C	7	0	0	0	0
Harold Jackson	D	3	0	0	0	0
Roger Jenkins	D	37	1	8	9	26
Virgil Johnson	D	25	0	2	2	2
Mike Karakas	G	48	2.80 GAA	0	0	0
Bill Kendall	RW	9	0	1	1	2
Alex Levinsky	D	48	3	2	5	18
Bill MacKenzie	D	35	1	2	3	20
Harold March	RW	42	11	17	28	16
Hickey Nicholson	LW	2	1	0	1	0
Pete Palangio	LW	19	2	1	3	4
Elwin Romnes	C	44	10	22	32	4
Earl Seibert	D/RW	48	8	13	21	38
Jack Shill	C	23	4	3	7	8
Paul Thompson	LW	48	22	22	44	14
Louis Trudel	RW	42	6	16	22	15
Carl Voss	C	34	3	8	11	0
Art Wiebe	D	43	0	3	3	24

Regular season statistics. Source: Chicago Blackhawks Media Guide

CHAPTER 6

The Miracle Makers

I n 1937–38, newly appointed coach Bill Stewart led a Blackhawks team that included many standout players. Seven of them (Johnny Gottselig; Roger Jenkins, who rejoined the team early in the season; Bill Kendall; Mush March; Doc Romnes; Paul Thompson; and Louis Trudel) were members of Chicago's 1933–34 Stanley Cup team. The roster also featured some new names, including goaltender Mike Karakas; defensemen Virgil Johnson, Earl Seibert, Bill MacKenzie, Alex Levinsky, and Art Wiebe; and forwards Cully Dahlstrom, Jack Shill, and Carl Voss.

Reflecting Frederic McLaughlin's obsession with having a completely American hockey team, Dahlstrom, Jenkins, Johnson, Karakas, Levinsky, Trudel, Voss, and Romnes were all American-born players. (Karakas, Dahlstrom, Romnes, and Johnson were both American-born and developed players, while Voss, Trudel, Jenkins, and Levinsky were really Canadian players who happened to be born in the United States.) Karakas had been coached by U.S. Hockey Hall of Famer Cliff Thompson at Eveleth High School in Minnesota. From 1920 to 1958, Thompson had a 534-26-9 record and took four of his teams to victory at the Minnesota state championship. He also coached at Eveleth Junior College. Eleven of the players he coached as youngsters (including Frank Brimsek, Mike Karakas, Sam LoPresti, and John Mariucci) played in the NHL, and a few competed in the Olympics.

(opposite) Cully Dahlstrom. (Photo courtesy of the Cully Dahlstrom family)

Art Wiebe, Bill MacKenzie, Cully Dahlstrom, Bill Thoms, and Mike Karakas line up for a photo in 1938. (Photo courtesy of the Art Wiebe family)

William J. "Bill" Stewart

Born in 1895 in Fitchburg, Massachusetts, Bill Stewart is one of the most colorful figures in American sports history. Although he was a dynamic presence in professional baseball and hockey, his connection to the latter sport was not formed at a young age. "All Bill Stewart learned about ice hockey as a boy came from playing shinny on Boston ponds," Gene Kessler explained in the February 5, 1938, issue of *Liberty Magazine*. "But even then ice was a side line. His specialty in the Everett high school was baseball, with track-running second."

Stewart's parents were very religious, according to his grandson, Bill Stewart III. "The fact that he was an athlete growing up was abhorrent to them," he said. "He used to win medals for track. He'd bring them home and one day his dad, who was a silversmith, melted them down and made doorstops out of them."

In baseball, Stewart mainly was a pitcher and an outfielder, excelling enough at the sport to attract scouts and go pro with the old New

England League's team in Brockton, Massachusetts, in 1913. Later, while playing in the U.S. Navy, Stewart's 16-1 record led to a contract to play for the Chicago White Sox in 1919. However, after attending spring training and playing in some exhibition games, he spent the regular season in Louisville.

Stewart took a break from professional baseball for five years. During that stint, some of his time was devoted to coaching baseball at Harvard and scouting for the Boston Red Sox. He finished his career as playing manager of the Eastern League's Waterbury Brasscos in 1928 and turned to officiating. After umpiring in the International and New York-Penn Leagues, Stewart advanced to the National League in 1933. He continued umpiring in the major leagues through 1954, officiating 3,192 regular-season games, 23 World Series games, and four All-Star contests.

Stewart complemented his baseball work by officiating hockey games, although he was a relative latecomer to the sport. "My grandfather didn't play in high school," Bill Stewart III explained. "He didn't start playing until after World War I. He got a job from George Brown, owner of the Boston Arena. This was prior to the Boston Garden. He was one of the assistant general managers, picked up skating, and started playing. . . . We have a picture of him in old goalie pads in the cellar of the old Boston Arena, circa 1921–22."

Stewart ultimately began coaching in his native Massachusetts. In addition to women's hockey at Radcliffe College, he coached Milton Academy for three seasons (1927–29) and MIT for six (1925–31). Stewart officiated college hockey games between Ivy League schools like Harvard and Princeton during the early 1920s. By 1926–27, he was refereeing games in the Canadian-American Hockey League (Can-Am), where he eventually became head referee.

After officiating occasionally for the National Hockey League since 1928, Stewart secured a full-time NHL refereeing appointment in November 1931 and eventually became referee-in-chief. "The National Hockey League only played on specific nights, obviously set by the train schedule," Bill Stewart III explained. "On the nights he wasn't working [there], he'd work in the American League, or in the Can-Am League prior to the American League, and [he] worked college hockey on other nights."

Stewart was as tough as they came. Former NHL referee Paul Stewart once explained that his grandfather was not the type of man to be intimidated. "He was the first guy to throw Jackie Robinson out of a game, he was the first guy to ever throw The Rocket [Maurice Richard] out of a game. So, it was in his makeup. He was right when he was right and was a man of his convictions."

It was Stewart's demeanor that landed him a coaching job with the Blackhawks. "They knew my grandfather," said Bill Stewart III. "They knew his reputation because he had come from refereeing. One of the reasons he got hired was because somebody threatened him one night when Major McLaughlin was there. He told this one off and told that one off, and [said] you can have my job if you want it, but that's the way it is. McLaughlin liked his stern attitude and steadfastness, which eventually got him fired."

In a March 25, 1962, *Chicago Tribune Magazine* article, Ted Damata elaborated on how McLaughlin hired Stewart after watching him umpire a game between the Cubs and St. Louis Cardinals in the summer of 1937. "Major McLaughlin's decision came at a precise moment that day in Wrigley field," he wrote. "The Gas House Gang had been riding Umpire Stewart over adverse decisions. Stewart called a strike on Joe [Ducky] Medwick, St. Louis slugger, and the Cardinal bench exploded. Stewart's Scotch ancestry was maligned. Umpire Stewart roared into action, banishing almost half the players from the game. That was when McLaughlin said, 'That's my man.'"

Stories of Stewart's steadfastness as a baseball umpire and NHL official are well documented. "In a New York-Pennsylvania League game he didn't hesitate to call a third strike on a home batter with the bases full and the score tied," explained a January 1, 1938, *Collier's* article. "He did that again on the second batter, and again on a third. Each batter refused to swing at good balls. After the game was over fifty hoodlums went at him, but he blazed a bare-fisted trail to the clubhouse.

"He watched a five-minute barrage of debris in Detroit two years ago and knew just how Joe Medwick felt in the World Series of a few months before. After the shower and noise had subsided, he went to the loudspeaker and challenged anybody to come down on the ice and throw something at him, preferably a fist.

Bill Stewart, likely at home, wearing his 1937–38 championship jacket. (Photo courtesy of the Boston Public Library, Leslie Jones Collection)

"A mob of 300 charged the dressing room in Montreal, and one knocked down the door-tender to gain entrance. Bill picked up the intruder and threw him bodily into the crowd. Then he stood at the end of a narrow alley and invited them to come along. In neither instance did anybody accept the offer."

During the 1930s, hockey officials received small salaries. In the event of illnesses or accidents, their contracts did not guarantee payment if they were unable to work a game. The same *Collier's* article described an incident where Stewart was injured while officiating a minor-league hockey game in Providence, Rhode Island. While attempting to shield himself from an airborne player, the triceps in Stewart's left arm was badly cut. He refused to let the injury keep him from officiating an upcoming Stanley Cup playoff game at Madison Square Garden.

"A couple of players happened to see the arm on the train and nearly fainted," the article explained. "It was twice normal size and blue from shoulder to wrist. From ten o'clock the next morning until five at night the doctors worked on that arm. And yet he refereed the Stanley Cup game in the Garden. He was lucky, though. He kept the arm close to his side and none of the players bodychecked him." (As a coach, Stewart refused to tolerate physical or verbal abuse of officials by his players).

Except for his time behind the Blackhawks' bench, Stewart was an NHL official from 1928 to 1941 when, to his surprise, the league released him from service. "Neither the Major nor his fanatically hockey-minded wife, Irene Castle McLaughlin, liked Bill Stewart as an N.H.L. referee," wrote Vern De Geer in the February 20, 1964, issue of Montreal's *Gazette*. "They frequently threatened to have him run out of the league after Hawk defeats at Chicago Stadium." After the NHL, Stewart's hockey career shifted to the AHL, where he became chief referee but remained for just one season.

When his career as a hockey official ended, Stewart continued working in professional baseball. According to a National Baseball Hall of Fame article by Matt Rothenberg, Stewart claimed that Commissioner Ford Frick had promised him a position to supervise the National League's umpires. When Warren Giles became National League president and eliminated the supervisory role, Stewart decided to end his officiating career.

Stewart's sports career had one more hockey-related highlight. In 1956, he was chosen to pilot the United States' national hockey team, which participated in the world championship tournament in March 1957. Although the U.S. State Department forced the team to withdraw from competition following the Soviet occupation of Hungary, Stewart and his players toured Europe, playing 25 exhibition games.

In later years, Stewart's involvement with baseball continued when he worked as a scout for both the Cleveland Indians and the Washington Senators. In his article, De Geer explained that Stewart also was a popular after-dinner speaker in both the United States and Canada. After suffering a stroke, Stewart died in February 1964, at age 69. He was inducted into the U.S. Hockey Hall of Fame in 1982.

Stewart's son, Bill Stewart, Jr., followed in his father's footsteps, coaching three high school sports and refereeing college football, hockey, and baseball games. The family's path through the sports world did not end there, however. Bill Stewart III also became an official, working three different sports at the college level. In December 2018,

Bill Stewart's grandson, Paul, a longtime NHL referee who officiated 1,010 regular-season games and 49 Stanley Cup playoff games between 1986 and 2003, joined him as a U.S. Hockey Hall of Fame inductee.

Carl Sidney "Cully" Dahlstrom

The son of Swedish immigrants, Carl "Cully" Dahlstrom began playing hockey at an early age, when he and his friends knocked cans around vacant lots with sticks. In an undated *Chicago Times* article he wrote to promote The TIMES Hockey School, a training program for young-sters held in Chicago's Garfield Park, Dahlstrom recalled his own youth hockey experience, commenting: "I started skating up in Minneapo-lis as early as any Canadian youngster. When I was only seven I used to hustle over to Riverside Park, which was one block from our home. There I skated with other kids of my age for hours at a time."

Dahlstrom did not play organized hockey until age 12. "A group of us formed a team and we entered the Minneapolis park system's junior league," he recalled. "We played so often and finally became so good that we could beat most of the teams in the park's junior league." After graduating at the top of his class at Minneapolis South High School in January 1930, Dahlstrom played hockey with Pillsbury and the Swed-ish Vikings of the Amateur Athletic Union. The Great Depression pre-vented him from pursuing a college education.

Soon, Dahlstrom got his big break. "Lyle Wright, then manager of the Minneapolis rink, watched us one day and after our game asked me to try out for the Minneapolis amateur team," he wrote in the same *Chi-cago Times* article. "I finally made the grade, but not until I put in untold hours of practice to improve my game."

Dahlstrom turned pro with the Minneapolis Millers in 1931–32 and was given the nickname "Cully," after former Millers' player Cully Wilson. In Minneapolis, he helped his team win the CHL champion-ship in 1931–32 and 1933–34. "It was really a 'car-fare' league, almost semi-pro," he said in a May 19, 1982, *Times Advocate* article. "We didn't make much money, but what little we received came in handy in those tough economic times. I was 18 years old and tickled to be making a few dollars for playing hockey."

Carl Sidney "Cully" Dahlstrom

Birthplace:	Minneapolis, Minnesota
Born:	July 3, 1912
Died:	December 19, 1998
Position:	Center
Weight:	175
Height:	5'11"
Chicago Blackhawks Stats	
Uniform #:	15, 21
Games Played:	342
Goals:	88
Assists:	118
Points:	206
Penalty Minutes:	58
Seasons:	1937–45
Scoring Leader (Goals):	1939–40 (11)
Scoring Leader (Assists):	1939–40 (19)
Scoring Leader (Total Points):	1939–40 (30)
Career Awards & Honors	
Awards:	Calder Memorial Trophy (Rookie of the Year) (1937–38)
U.S. Hockey Hall of Fame:	1973

Cully eventually began playing for the CHL's St. Paul Saints, who became part of the AHA in 1935–36. According to some accounts, he was sold, along with several other players, to St. Paul by Lyle Wright, who wanted to create a rivalry between the Twin Cities. Other sources indicate that Dahlstrom was traded following a salary dispute with Wright. In any case, he went on to become a top scorer, earning All-Star honors several times. Before long, Dahlstrom was invited to try out for the Boston Bruins, but things did not work out.

"I just didn't have the natural talent like some kids do today to jump directly to the NHL," he said in the May 24, 1985, issue of the *Hockey News*. "I can remember getting a tryout one year with the Boston Bruins and going to their training camp. After the first couple of days I realized that I wasn't ready to jump to the NHL yet. Those guys just skated circles around me. It was as though I was going in slow motion the way those players played. That's why it really didn't bother me when I went

Congratulatory telegram from NHL President Frank Calder to Cully Dahlstrom. (Photo courtesy of the Cully Dahlstrom family)

back to the minors. But when I got my tryout with the Blackhawks, that was a different story. Then I knew I was ready for the NHL."

After his unsuccessful Boston tryout, Cully was discovered by the Blackhawks while playing for St. Paul. "I kind of lost interest in possibly going to the National League," he recalled in 1993. "But then I got a call from Bill Tobin. He wanted me to come down to training camp [at the University of Illinois, Chicago]. . . . After a half a week of practice sessions, Tobin contacted me and wanted me to come down to the office. At that time, he offered me a contract and I said I couldn't accept it. So I negotiated a little higher, which was still peanuts. Then I signed the contract and went to training camp. I tried out and was successful. At least I made the team and started in the National League for the first game."

Dahlstrom ultimately received the Calder Trophy for being the NHL's best rookie. "This is honest," he said. "I thought there was a poor crop of rookies that year. I had no idea that I would be nominated for that position and accredited rookie of the year. But things happen, and

[they] happened well for me. I had read a little bit about it, but I didn't think I would be a winner in that category."

Some considered Dahlstrom one of the game's best forecheckers due to his roving style of play. Thinking back to the many hours he spent on the ice, Cully once described the type of player he was. "As an athlete, I also played in other sports," he said. "I played softball (third base) and we went to the finals in the National Softball Tournament. In hockey, I played an all-around center position. I was good on defense. As a matter of fact, I did many, many terms of playing shorthanded for the club. So, I was good defensively and reasonably good offensively, but not as good as some of 'em."

In 1973, Dahlstrom was among the first group of United States Hockey Hall of Fame inductees, along with former Chicago teammate and fellow Calder Trophy winner Mike Karakas. Following hockey, he pursued a career in real estate, working as an appraiser, broker, builder, and developer in Bellevue, Washington. After living in Escondido, California, for nearly 20 years, he moved back to Bellevue in 1995, where he passed away three years later.

Virgil Sylvester Johnson

Virgil Johnson was one of several American-born players on Chicago's roster in 1937–38. Raised in the North Minneapolis neighborhood of Camden, he played baseball, football, and hockey in high school. Johnson turned down athletic scholarships from Notre Dame and the University of Minnesota to pursue a career in professional hockey.

Following an unsuccessful tryout with the Blackhawks in 1931, Johnson's professional career began as a defenseman for the Minneapolis Millers (CHL), where he was a fan favorite from 1931–34. Johnson joined the CHL's St. Paul Saints in 1934–35 (the Saints switched to the AHA the following season). He made the Blackhawks' roster in 1937–38 and contributed to the team's second Stanley Cup victory. Johnson then returned to St. Paul for four seasons, earning Most Valuable Player honors in 1942.

After playing for the Hershey Bears (AHL) in 1942–43, Johnson returned to the Blackhawks from 1943–45. Following stints with the AHL's Cleveland Barons and the United States Pro Hockey League's (USHL)

Virgil Sylvester Johnson

Birthplace:	Minneapolis, Minnesota
Born:	March 4, 1912
Died:	September 9, 1993
Position:	Defense
Weight:	165
Height:	5'8"
Chicago Blackhawks Stats	
Uniform #:	10, 18, 19
Games Played:	75
Goals:	2
Assists:	9
Points:	11
Penalty Minutes:	27
Seasons:	1937–38, 1943–45
Career Awards & Honors	
U.S. Hockey Hall of Fame:	1974

Minneapolis Millers, he did not play from 1947–50. Johnson's career ended in the All-American Hockey League (AAHL), where he skated for the Minneapolis Jerseys in 1950–51 and the St. Paul Saints in 1951–52.

While not the bone-crushing variety of defenseman, Johnson was dangerous in rushing situations because of his speed and bodychecking abilities. He also was good at taking close shots and was an accurate passer. According to the official Virgil Johnson website, Johnny Mariucci, who played for the Blackhawks in the 1940s, said the following of Virgil during his October 26, 1974, United States Hockey Hall of Fame induction: "He was one of the smallest defensemen in the league, but very effective. He was a magician with his stick. He was like a terrier after a rat when he moved in and stole the puck. He could do it against the best stick handlers."

Michael "Iron Mike" Karakas

Mike Karakas learned to play hockey in Eveleth, Minnesota, in a flooded lot near the Spruce Mine with other sons of Oliver Iron Mining Company workers. "They were poor," recalls his daughter, Joan Karakas. "In the beginning, he had to wear his sister Kate's double runners. His face would just go crimson when you even mentioned it. Finally, he graduated and got his own pair of skates."

Karakas spent three years playing on the Eveleth High School team, and while attending junior college played for the Eveleth Rangers (CHL) in 1929–30. He was a backup goalie for the AHA's Chicago Shamrocks in 1930–31 and became the team's regular netminder the following season, when he was named the AHA's most valuable goalie. While playing for the Shamrocks, Karakas spent much of his free time at Chicago Stadium, watching the legendary Chuck Gardiner tend goal in practice and competition, and learning how to emulate Gardiner's style and technique.

After stints with AHA teams in St. Louis and Tulsa, Karakas found himself in a difficult spot, according to a December 10, 1938, *Collier's* article. "Hard luck and failure dogged his heels," it explained. "Clubs were sold from under him. Whole leagues were abandoned, and one goaltending job after another vanished. Those setbacks always hit a kid of twenty-three harder when he has a wife and baby back in the home town, waiting for him to make good on promises of gold and glory in professional hockey."

Although he had escaped the attention of NHL team managers and owners, Karakas sent a letter to Frederic McLaughlin, appealing for a chance to play for the Blackhawks. At the time, conventional thinking was that talented goaltenders came from Canada, not the United States. In the eyes of many, no one would ever hold a candle to the legendary Chuck Gardiner.

Even so, in early October Karakas received a telegram instructing him to report to the Blackhawks' training camp in Urbana, Illinois, where he was greeted by coach Clem Loughlin. Because Karakas's equipment was still in Tulsa, Loughlin told him to wear Chuck Gardiner's old gear, which the team still had. When Lorne Chabot was injured during training camp, Karakas became the Blackhawks' goaltender in 1935–36. To McLaughlin's excitement, he also was the first American-born goalie to play in the NHL.

"Skating onto the Chicago Stadium ice for the opening game, Mike felt that he was carrying some kind of sacred heritage," *Collier's* ex-

Michael "Iron Mike" Karakas

Birthplace:	Aurora, Minnesota
Born:	December 12, 1911
Died:	May 2, 1992
Position:	Goaltender
Weight:	147
Height:	5'11"
Chicago Blackhawks Stats	
Uniform #:	1, 18
Games Played:	331
Goals Against Average:	2.91
Shutouts:	28
Penalty Minutes:	9
Seasons:	1935–40, 1943–46
Career Awards & Honors	
Awards:	Calder Memorial Trophy (Rookie of the Year) (1935–36)
All-Star (Second Team):	1944–45
U.S. Hockey Hall of Fame:	1973

plained. "Of course, it was the weight of Chuck Gardiner's equipment. The club had new red, black and white uniforms, but Mike, kidlike, had stuck to Gardiner's shoulder harness, pads, and gloves. They made him feel like a better goalie. So did that great Stadium organ as it boomed out the rousing Indian melody. The capacity crowd roared and it was like living through a dream.

"A few minutes later his ears were burning from a gigantic chorus of razzberries, and he was fishing a puck from the nets. The New York Americans had scored, despite the sacred equipment and all the inspiration. After that Mike settled down to more material hockey, and held the Americans scoreless while his mates were jamming home three goals to give him his first big-league victory."

During his first season in Chicago, Karakas registered nine shutouts and a 1.85 goals-against average, earning top rookie honors. With the Blackhawks, Karakas's career goals-against average was 2.91 and he allowed only 15 goals during the 1937–38 Stanley Cup playoffs. "He was always a good goalie," former Blackhawks forward Cully Dahlstrom once recalled. "We thought we had the best goalie in the league."

A profile of Karakas in *30 Memorable Games Played by Chicago's Black Hawks* called him "a cool workman in the nets" who was "adroit at passing the puck to his mates." On February 21, 1945, Karakas became the fifth goalie in NHL history to be credited with an assist. After Georges Vezina (1918–19), other acclaimed netminders who accomplished this feat included John Ross Roach (1930–31), Tiny Thompson (1935–36), and Bert Gardiner (1943–44).

Joan Karakas confirmed her father's "cool workman" status, explaining: "I was very young when I saw him play, but he always would present a very calm image. I'm sure it had to be nerve-racking, but he would never present that. Even with family things, the things that come up in life that are serious and scary, he always kept a calm exterior. Inside he might be falling apart, but you would see the strong kind of quiet type."

Elaborating on her father's character, Joan said: "My father never swore. He wasn't a drinker. People think hockey guys are tough guys, but he was a very clean-living person. He was a very good person. I'm not trying to make a saint out of him or anything. He was a regular guy, but he was, I think, very decent."

The first leg of Karakas's career with Chicago ended in 1939–40, and he rounded out that season playing five games for the Montreal Canadiens. After three seasons in the AHL, where he played for the Providence Reds, New Haven Eagles, and Springfield Indians, Karakas returned to Chicago in 1943–44 and took the Blackhawks to the Stanley Cup finals against the Habs (the Canadiens' nickname, an abbreviation of "Les Habitants"), where they lost. In 1944–45, he led the NHL in shutouts, along with Toronto's Frank McCool, and was named to the second All-Star team. After 1945–46, Karakas returned to the AHL and finished his career in Providence. Following hockey, he worked as a commercial fisherman and carpenter.

Alexander "Alex" "Mine Boy" Levinsky

Alex Levinsky was a solid role player at the blue line for the Blackhawks during the last half of the 1930s. Among the NHL's first American-born Jewish hockey players (and the first professional hockey player born in

Syracuse, New York), his family relocated to Toronto when he was still very young. Levinsky earned the nickname "Mine Boy" because his parents would shout, "That's Mine Boy," from the stands during his games.

While playing junior and senior hockey for the Ontario Hockey Association's (OHA) Toronto Marlboros, Levinsky caught the eye of Conn Smythe, who owned both the Marlboros and the Maple Leafs, and made the latter team's roster in March 1931. He faced off against the Blackhawks during the first game ever played in Maple Leaf Gardens on November 12, 1931, a 2-1 loss to Chicago, and helped his team win the Stanley Cup that season (1931–32).

In a trade that some sources attribute to anti-Semitism on the part of Smythe, the Maple Leafs traded Levinsky to the New York Rangers in April 1934. Despite being one of the NHL's better defensemen, his opportunities were limited in the Big Apple. The Rangers already had top blue-liners like Ching Johnson and Earl Seibert on their roster, limiting Levinsky's ice time.

After 20 games with the Rangers, the Blackhawks picked up Levinsky. He remained in Chicago until 1938–39, playing almost 200 games. Levinsky's career ended in 1940 with the IAHL's Philadelphia Ramblers.

Alexander "Alex" "Mine Boy" Levinsky

Birthplace:	Syracuse, New York
Born:	February 2, 1910
Died:	September 1, 1990
Position:	Defense
Weight:	184
Height:	5'10"
Chicago Blackhawks Stats	
Uniform #:	8
Games Played:	197
Goals:	8
Assists:	24
Points:	32
Penalty Minutes:	171
Seasons:	1934–39

This November 7, 1935, *Chicago Daily Times* photo shows Chicago's goal from the opposition's perspective during the 1930s. Defensemen Alex Levinsky (left) and Art Wiebe (right) defend goalie Mike Karakas. (Photo courtesy of the Art Wiebe family)

William Kenneth "Bill" MacKenzie

Winnipeg native Bill MacKenzie was an effective role player for Chicago in 1937–38. As captain of the Elmwood Millionaires (City Jr.), he helped his team win the Memorial Cup in 1931. After two seasons with the Millionaires (1929–31), MacKenzie played senior hockey for the Montreal City Hockey League's (MCHL) Montreal AAA in 1931–32. He entered the NHL with Chicago the following season, also playing 12 games in the MCHL for the Montreal Royals.

Although he played defense and focused on getting the puck to forwards, some sources credit MacKenzie with having a good shot from the point. After the Blackhawks released MacKenzie in July 1933, he played for the Montreal Maroons, New York Rangers, Windsor Bulldogs (IAHL), and Montreal Canadiens. He rejoined the Blackhawks on December 10, 1937, in a trade for Marty Burke. MacKenzie ended his NHL career, which spanned nearly 300 games, in 1940.

William Kenneth "Bill" MacKenzie

Birthplace:	Winnipeg, Manitoba
Born:	December 12, 1911
Died:	May 29, 1990
Position:	Defense
Weight:	175
Height:	5'11"
Chicago Blackhawks Stats	
Uniform #:	4, 9
Games Played:	101
Goals:	2
Assists:	3
Points:	5
Penalty Minutes:	70
Seasons:	1932–33, 1937–40
Career Awards & Honors	
Manitoba Hockey Hall of Fame:	1985

When his NHL days were over, MacKenzie played for the Cleveland Barons, who won the AHL championship in 1941. His AHL career was interrupted by service in World War II in 1943–44. However, MacKenzie returned to the Barons the following season, playing the final 13 games of his professional career.

After playing, MacKenzie coached junior hockey, first in the Manitoba Junior Hockey League, where he led the Brandon Wheat Kings to the Memorial Cup finals in 1949. Later, MacKenzie coached senior amateur hockey's Kelowna Packers in the Mainline-Okanagan Hockey League.

Earl Walter "Big Dutchman" Seibert

Earl Seibert played junior hockey for the OHA's Kitchener Greenshirts from 1927–29. During two seasons with the Can-Am League's Springfield Indians, he suffered a serious concussion, after which he became one of the first players to regularly wear protective headgear. Seibert broke into the NHL with the New York Rangers in 1931–32, joining fellow defensemen Ivan "Ching" Johnson and Ehrhardt "Ott" Heller. On January 15, 1936, the Rangers traded him to the Blackhawks for Art Coulter.

In addition to scoring power, tremendous speed, and the ability to effectively block shots from opposing players, Seibert was a dominating force because of his physical size. Former Blackhawks employee John Robertson, who began working for the team during the late 1930s, said Seibert was one of the strongest men he ever saw. At 6'2", Seibert weighed anywhere between 198 and 220 pounds throughout his career, making him an imposing presence on the ice and earning him nicknames like the Big Dutchman.

A profile in 30 Memorable Games Played by Chicago's Black Hawks called Seibert "a bone-crusher of the first degree" and explained that he "was regarded as a 'policeman' on ice, and was the avenger of the wrongs done to younger and smaller team members." Feared NHL tough guys like Toronto's Red Horner and Boston's Eddie Shore supposedly avoided entanglements with Seibert whenever possible. According to a December 31, 2007, article in Montreal's Gazette, Shore once commented: "It's lucky he was a calm boy. If he ever got mad, he'd have killed us all."

Former Detroit Red Wings and Boston Bruins defenseman Bill Quackenbush, who was inducted into the Hockey Hall of Fame in 1976, said Seibert was the toughest player he ever faced in the NHL. "[He was] one of the best defensemen ever to play the game," Quackenbush recalled in 1996. "He was a one-man team with Chicago."

Seibert led all NHL defensemen in scoring in 1933–34. A fan favorite in Chicago, during the team's 1937–38 championship season he was on the ice almost constantly, contributing heavily to the club's second Stanley Cup victory. Seibert was given All-Star honors in 10 consecutive seasons.

While playing for the Blackhawks, Seibert experienced a setback that would haunt him for the rest of his life. During a game against the Montreal Canadiens on January 28, 1937, he checked Howie Morenz behind the Chicago net. Although it was a clean check, Morenz fell, shattering his leg in four places. Sadly, he died from a pulmonary embolism six weeks later.

During his career, Seibert was overshadowed by Eddie Shore, even though some considered Seibert to be the better player. In a February 17, 1995, Hockey News article, Richard Beals wrote: "though he was a

Earl Walter "Big Dutchman" Seibert

Birthplace:	Kitchener, Ontario
Born:	December 7, 1911
Died:	May 12, 1990
Position:	Defense
Weight:	198
Height:	6'2"
Chicago Blackhawks Stats	
Uniform #:	17
Games Played:	477
Goals:	57
Assists:	131
Points:	188
Penalty Minutes:	387
Seasons:	1935–45
Team Captain:	1940–42
Career Awards & Honors	
All-Star (First Team):	1934–35, 1941–42, 1942–43, 1943–44
All-Star (Second Team):	1935–36, 1936–37, 1937–38, 1938–39, 1939–40, 1940–41
Hockey Hall of Fame:	1963

gentle man, Seibert's stubbornness and perceived mercenary attitude rubbed a few people the wrong way."

In the same article, Seibert's former Chicago Blackhawks and New York Rangers teammate Clint Smith explained: "The only thing about Earl was that he decided when he wanted to play and when he didn't. His attitude was his worst enemy. He decided if they were only going to pay him $7,500, that's all [they were] going to get out of him. If [he played] like Eddie Shore, 100 percent every night, he could have been one of the greats."

Nevertheless, Seibert is credited for being a positive influence on his teammates. A Hockey Hall of Fame (HHOF) profile mentions his serious demeanor and credits him for "mature play and tremendous leadership." In the same 30 Memorable Games article, the Blackhawks remembered him as "a great leader and inspirational force on the team."

Seibert's HHOF profile claims that he was offered an ownership stake in the Blackhawks by Frederic McLaughlin, who was extremely

Mary Ann
~~~ & Wishes
~~~ Best of Luck
Sincerely
~~~ Seibert
Feb 22/37

Earl Seibert in the doorway of Art Wiebe's Guyon Hotel apartment. (Photo courtesy of the Art Wiebe family)

fond of the Big Dutchman. However, manager Bill Tobin refused to recognize the deal following McLaughlin's death. After his playing career ended, Seibert was coach and co-owner of the American League's Springfield Indians with his formal rival, Eddie Shore. When the relationship soured and his affiliation with the Indians ended in 1951, Seibert walked away from the game for good.

Seibert's father, Oliver, was inducted into the Hockey Hall of Fame in 1961. When Earl was inducted two years later, Earl and Oliver became the very first father and son inductees. Rather than attend his induction ceremony, Seibert stayed home. He lived his last years in Agawam, Massachusetts, where he owned a liquor store, before dying from cancer at age 78. Eddie Shore's son, Ted, paid his respects to Earl at the Agawam Funeral Home. His father had died five years before.

(opposite) Defenseman Earl Seibert. (Photo courtesy of the Art Wiebe family)

John Walker "Jack" "Snowball" Shill

Jack Shill's hockey career began in 1929 with the junior Toronto Marlboros (OHA). He saw his first NHL action in 1933–34, playing a handful of games for the Toronto Maple Leafs. Throughout Shill's long career, he played for many senior and minor-league clubs, including the Boston Cubs (Can-Am) and Syracuse Stars (IAHL), and saw NHL action during stints with the Maple Leafs, Boston Bruins, and New York Americans.

Jack, whose premature balding earned him the nickname "Snowball," arrived in Chicago on January 26, 1938, when the Blackhawks paid cash for him in a deal with the Americans. Although he was a role player, Shill did his part in contributing to the Windy City's second Stanley Cup victory. However, the Blackhawks were the last NHL club that Shill played for.

On October 24, 1939, the Blackhawks sold Shill to the Providence Reds (IAHL/AHL), where he became a star player. There, Shill participated in the very first AHL All-Star Game in 1942. During the 1940s, he also played for several Toronto and District Senior Hockey Leagues (Tor-Sr.) teams, including the Toronto Research Colonels, Toronto Dehavillands, Toronto Tip Tops, and Toronto Maher Jewels.

John Walker "Jack" "Snowball" Shill

Birthplace:	Toronto, Ontario
Born:	January 12, 1913
Died:	October 25, 1976
Positions:	Defense, Left Wing, Center
Weight:	175
Height:	5' 9"
Chicago Blackhawks Stats	
Uniform #:	3
Games Played:	51
Goals:	6
Assists:	7
Points:	13
Penalty Minutes:	12
Seasons:	1937–39

Shill was not the only NHL player in his family. His brother, William Roy "Bill" Shill, played for the Boston Bruins during the 1940s. After suffering a back injury on December 8, 1948, in a game between the Maher Jewels and the Toronto Barkers, Shill's hockey career came to an end. In later years, he worked for the City of Toronto.

Carl Potter Voss

Born in Chelsea, Massachusetts, Carl Voss eventually relocated to Canada, where his hockey career began in 1925–26 with the Ontario Hockey Association Senior A (OHA Sr.) Kingston Frontenacs, who won the Memorial Cup that season. Voss also played halfback for the Queen's University football team that year. After joining the OHA's Toronto Marlboros, Voss went pro with the Toronto Maple Leafs, playing 12 games in 1926–27. According to the Hockey Hall of Fame, he was the first Maple Leafs player signed by team owner Conn Smythe.

Carl Potter Voss

Birthplace:	Chelsea, Massachusetts
Born:	January 6, 1907
Died:	September 13, 1993
Position:	Center
Weight:	168
Height:	5'9"
Chicago Blackhawks Stats	
Uniform #:	14
Games Played:	34
Goals:	3
Assists:	8
Points:	11
Penalty Minutes:	0
Seasons:	1937–38
Career Awards & Honors	
Awards:	Calder Memorial Trophy (Rookie of the Year) (1932–33)
Hockey Hall of Fame:	1974 (Builder)

During the early part of his career, Voss mainly played for minor-league teams like the Canadian Professional Hockey League's (Can-Pro) Toronto Falcons and London Panthers, and the IAHL's Buffalo Bisons, helping the latter team win a league championship in 1932. That year, he received All-Star (first team) honors and led the IAHL in scoring. Voss became an NHL regular in 1932–33 when he joined the New York Rangers. After playing in only 10 games for New York, he was traded to the Detroit Red Wings, earning rookie-of-the-year honors as the very first player to receive the Calder Memorial Trophy.

When his time in the Motor City ended in 1933–34, Voss played for other NHL teams during the 1930s, including the Ottawa Senators, St. Louis Eagles, New York Americans, and Montreal Maroons. He signed with the Blackhawks as a free agent on December 6, 1937, and contributed to the team's Stanley Cup victory in 1938. After injuring his knee that season, Voss made an unsuccessful attempt to play the following year, but hung up the skates on September 30, 1938, in training camp.

After playing, Voss's involvement with the sport of hockey was far from over. He refereed both college and minor-league games, moved into a supervisory role, and ultimately became president of the USHL. Voss was named NHL referee-in-chief in 1950, and during the next 15 years made a significant impact on the quality of NHL officiating. In 1974, he was inducted into the Hockey Hall of Fame as a builder.

Arthur Walter Ronald "Art" Wiebe

Art Wiebe began playing hockey on local ponds before joining town and school teams in Vermilion, Alberta. His first major break came at age 17 while playing in a provincial junior championship. Influential coach Barney Stanley—a former professional player who coached the Blackhawks in 1927–28 and also scouted for the team—saw Wiebe's performance and recruited him to play junior hockey for the Edmonton Poolers (City Jr.), where he joined future Tulsa Oilers and Chicago Blackhawks teammate Louis Trudel. The Poolers took their name from the Northern Alberta Dairy Pool, where Stanley was employed.

The March 1, 1935, *Edmonton Journal* called Wiebe a "fast skater and

Arthur Walter Ronald "Art" Wiebe

Birthplace:	Rosthern, Saskatchewan
Born:	September 28, 1912
Died:	June 6, 1971
Position:	Defense
Weight:	180
Height:	5'10"
Chicago Blackhawks Stats	
Uniform #:	2, 10, 11
Games Played:	414
Goals:	14
Assists:	27
Points:	41
Penalty Minutes:	201
Seasons:	1932–44

a 'rusher' of more than ordinary merit from the start," explaining that he "gave junior fans many a thrill at the Arena in the two seasons he was with Stanley's team."

In January 1936, *Edmonton Journal* sportswriter Tommy Graham said that "Art's particular style of play proved pleasing to the fans almost overnight, and it was not long before he was one of the most popular players in the junior loop. He used to wow 'em with his rushes which reminded you of a charging bull ready to jab his horns into the victim. He would just plow down the ice as fast as his sturdy legs would carry him, and, although this was not very fast, he always managed to get there and accounted for his share of goals during the season's play. But it was on defense that Art really starred."

Wiebe's professional career began in 1932–33 when he was signed by the Blackhawks. "Mr. Stanley noticed one scout after another looking at this young teenager so he advised the Chicago organization to sign him right away," recalled *Edmonton Journal* sportswriter Tiger Goldstick in 1971. "At the Chicago training camp he looked good and he drew rave notices from the sports media, players and coaches alike."

Although Wiebe played four games for the big club, he ultimately was assigned to the St. Paul Greyhounds (AHA), which relocated and

The 1931–32 Edmonton Poolers were Northern Alberta Junior Hockey Champions. Top row (left to right): Alf Walker, Eddie Franks (trainer), Louis Trudel, Art Wiebe, Art Potter (manager), Ab Miniely, Bob Gillies, Barney Stanley (coach), and Ab Darkes. Bottom row (left to right): Neil Colville, Andy Maloney, George McClintock, Harry Maloney, and Howard Smith. (Photo courtesy of the Art Wiebe family)

became the Tulsa Oilers. Instead of finishing the season in Tulsa, Wiebe was transferred to the Kansas City Greyhounds, which won the AHA championship in 1933–34.

A clipping from Wiebe's scrapbook, likely taken from a Greyhounds game program, provided the following description of him during his time in Kansas City: "If there ever was a real honest-to-goodness fellow, this courageous defense man and jolting body-checker, Art Wiebe, is entitled to the honor. With a stick in his hand he is a human torpedo that can create more bitter rivalry than any other player."

Destined to join the Blackhawks, Wiebe became a regular member of the team's lineup in 1934–35. In the Windy City, he quickly gained the admiration of fellow players, President Bill Tobin, and owner Frederic McLaughlin. During the 1930s and 1940s, Wiebe and teammate Earl Seibert formed one of the NHL's most formidable defensive duos.

This photo of defenseman Art Wiebe appeared on his rookie card. (Photo courtesy of the Art Wiebe family)

The *Edmonton Journal*'s Tommy Graham described the attributes that made Wiebe a solid NHL defenseman. "Physically, Wiebe is constructed in a robust manner," he wrote in January 1936. "His shoulders are reasonably compact but no one would ever believe that he tips the scales at 192 pounds. That is because he carries most of his weight in his legs. They are tremendous, so large in fact they give him a rather underslung appearance. But they are mighty powerful and undoubtedly account for his durability and rugged style of play while in action. It takes plenty to knock Art off his pins . . . and when he hits you he sure jars you with a powerful jolt that isn't easy to get over in a hurry."

In March 1939, sportswriter Edwin MC K. Johnson touted Wiebe as the "hottest defense man in the National Hockey League." Noting his exceptional bodychecking abilities, Johnson called Wiebe the Blackhawks' "unsung torpedo" and described how his defensive performance in a March 5, 1939, game against the Montreal Canadiens (a 2-1 overtime loss) caught everyone's attention, including team manager

Earl Seibert and Art Wiebe (2) play defense against the New York Rangers in 1936. (Photo courtesy of the Art Wiebe family)

Paul Thompson, who claimed it was the best he had seen in 13 years.

In attendance that night was F. W. "Nick" Kahler, a Minnesota Sports Hall of Fame inductee who once owned the Minneapolis Millers. "He was out there popping 'em," Kahler said in Johnson's article. "He's like the old-timers, Buz Murray, birds like that who never missed 'em. When he came into a guy, he just whammed him down. He didn't miss any of them and he gave Toe Blake, who charged in like a demon, one tough night. Wiebe's aggressive checking makes forwards come in with their heads up—slows the attack. Any time a defense man keeps cocking 'em like Wiebe, he's a hockey player. It was the nicest exhibition of defense play I've seen in years. And to think I could have bought him for a song a couple years ago!"

During his career, Wiebe played 414 games for the Blackhawks. In addition to hockey, he excelled at golf and curling. Wiebe briefly retired in 1942 and 1943 to run a bakery in Vermilion, Alberta, but was coaxed back into service on both occasions by Blackhawks manager Bill Tobin.

"When Art retired in the 40's many players will tell you that he could have played for several more seasons," recalled Goldstick. "Just for him to be on the ice with the team or in the dressing room he would give any club a lift. Because he was such a great competitor the rookies all looked up to him for help and believe me he helped plenty."

Wiebe's competitive spirit was not the only thing that younger players took notice of in the locker room. "He played to win but when he lost he was such a good sport he went out of his way to congratulate the winner," said Goldstick. "Art was always a winner because he did so much for sport[s]."

The quality of Wiebe's character left an impression on teammates and family members alike. "During the 12 years that I knew my grandfather, I remember a big man with a big heart," says his grandson, Mark Hemstock. "My grandparents lived just a few blocks from our home, and we were always getting together to share a meal and celebrate special occasions. One Christmas, we sang Christmas songs as a group and as individuals and made recordings on a cassette tape. My grandfather made a recording, but he was laughing so hard he could not finish the song."

Hemstock credits his grandparents for buying his first set of hockey equipment and remembers them watching him play on a cold outdoor rink. Wiebe's friendship with a fellow hockey legend made a community celebration extra special in 1967. "Gordie Howe came to our neighborhood to officially open the new community playground facility," recalls Hemstock. "My grandfather and Gordie were friends and they shared a few golf games together, so it was perhaps no coincidence that Gordie visited our neighborhood."

After playing, Wiebe coached the University of Alberta Golden Bears from 1950 to 1953, leading them to a Canada West title in 1951. Later, he became president of Regent Drilling Ltd., while also managing his family farm. Wiebe died in 1971, following a struggle with cancer. In 1971–72, the first Art Wiebe Memorial Trophy was awarded to a hockey player in Vermilion, Alberta.

The University of Alberta Golden Bears hockey team received a visit from Hollywood celebrity Bob Hope (holding stick) in 1950–51. Coach Art Wiebe stands to Hope's left. (Photo courtesy of the Art Wiebe family)

CHAPTER 7

An Umpire Shall Lead Them

The National Hockey League consisted of eight teams in 1937–38. The Blackhawks were in the American Division, along with the Boston Bruins, New York Rangers, and Detroit Red Wings. The Canadian Division included the Toronto Maple Leafs, New York Americans, Montreal Canadiens, and Montreal Maroons. "Competition was tough at that time because there were fewer teams," recalled Cully Dahlstrom.

As Chicago prepared for another hockey season, some players and fans likely questioned owner Frederic McLaughlin's decision to replace head coach Clem Loughlin with baseball umpire and NHL referee Bill Stewart. The January 1, 1938, issue of *Collier's* described 42-year-old Stewart as "a sad-faced gent whose heavy-lidded, blue-gray eyes make him look as though he has been reversed on every decision. Across the top of his pate are brushed the last stubborn strands of his hair. The only suggestion of his calling is a long, determined chin. His tastes are few and simple, and he stops at the smaller, secluded hotels. He carries a tiny radio set, a trunk that looks ready to fall apart and a trick chest protector which he himself fashioned out of a set of football shoulder pads and sponge rubber."

Virgil Johnson (right) poses for a photo with friends Cully Dahlstrom (center) and Clifford "Fido" Purpur (left) in 1944. Purpur was a Blackhawks forward from 1941–45. (Photo courtesy of the Virgil Johnson family)

Stewart's reputation preceded him. While refereeing, he once ejected his predecessor from a game at Chicago Stadium. According to the same article, one of Stewart's calls angered Loughlin, who lost his temper. Angry words followed and Loughlin was about to get physical when Stewart banished him to the locker room for the rest of the game. "Somebody hastened to Stewart with the whispered news that Frank Calder, president of the Hockey League, was in a near-by box," the article explained. "'I'm running this game,' he replied. 'After it's over, Calder can fire me, if he wants to.' Instead of firing him, Calder eventually made Stewart referee in chief of the league, quite an honor for a non-Canadian."

Training Camp

Before heading to training camp in Muskegon, Michigan, some of the Blackhawks engaged in early workouts at the Victor F. Lawson House YMCA, a 24-story Art Deco building at the northeast corner of West Chicago Avenue and Dearborn Street in the city's Near North Side neighborhood. Glenn Brydson, Bill Kendall, Alex Levinsky, Pete Palangio, Earl Seibert, Louis Trudel, and Art Wiebe underwent 10 days of gym conditioning there. They were among 18 players to arrive at the Muskegon Mart Auditorium for the start of camp on Saturday, October 9, 1937. In the absence of coach Stewart, who was busy umpiring a World Series game between the Yankees and Giants, veteran players took charge by running an evening skating drill.

The following morning, Blackhawks Vice President Bill Tobin oversaw an hour-long practice. He was pleased with the condition of the players, especially center Doc Romnes, who had been sidelined by a charley horse for 22 games the previous season. On October 12, defenseman Earl Seibert took a puck to the face, opening a gash close to his right eye. Although the injury required five stitches, he continued participating in drills. By the end of the week, Stewart had lined up several exhibition games against the Michigan-Ontario league's Muskegon Reds.

In the February 5, 1938, issue of *Liberty Magazine*, writer Gene Kessler touted Stewart's year-round work ethic in the sports of baseball and hockey. As the 1937 World Series concluded and Stewart arrived in Muskegon to take charge as Chicago's new coach, he had umpired 158 baseball games, including five in the World Series. The previous season, Stewart umpired 160 baseball games and officiated 69 hockey games as the NHL's referee in chief. This left little time for life at home, where his longest stretch was only 10 days.

During training camp, Stewart laid out his expectations for the players. "When we were in Muskegon for preseason training I told everyone how I felt about conditioning and drinking," he said in a March 28, 1960, *Sports Illustrated* article by Herm Weiskopf. "I told them they would have to get in shape and stay in shape if they wanted to win. I said I didn't mind if they had a few drinks, as long as it was not on the day of a game and not in public."

In the same article, Stewart reflected on the bonds he ultimately formed with his players throughout the upcoming season. "We were like one big, happy family," he said. "I used to joke a lot with the boys and sometimes I'd wrestle or box with them in the locker room."

With his officiating background, Stewart added a new twist to training camp on October 15, informing players that rule infractions, including offsides, would be enforced during scrimmages. In the October 16, 1937, *Chicago Daily Tribune*, he explained: "While refereeing, I have seen hundreds of well thought out attacking endeavors killed because the offside rule was broken. Half of the violations are unnecessary. Schooling the players in advance will minimize these infractions and establish better timing, thereby enhancing opportunities to score. That's the reason I'm making a map out of the ice surface. It's merely a kind of a speed indicator so that each forward can regulate his style and speed to the styles and speeds of his line mates."

Stewart's approach was sound, considering that the NHL made changes to the playing surface in 1937–38. That year, the face-off dot in front of each goal was removed and two new face-off dots were added in each defensive zone. To accommodate new icing rules, a goal line that spanned the entire width of the ice was added to each defensive zone, directly behind the goalie crease. The following season, each blue line became 12 inches wide.

Stewart was paying close attention to the team's defensemen, subjecting them to grueling workouts before the upcoming exhibition

EARLY CHICAGO SPORTSWRITERS IMPACT NHL

In Chicago, several talented writers brought sports to life in newsprint during the Great Depression. Some had a lasting impact on professional hockey. The *Chicago Tribune*'s Ted Damata was remembered as "the finest hockey writer this city ever knew, knows now, or will ever know" by sportswriter Bob Verdi in the paper's December 12, 1974, issue. Damata (1984) and Verdi (2016) are both winners of the Professional Hockey Writers Association's Elmer Ferguson Award for bringing honor to journalism and hockey.

Damata's career spanned six decades, beginning in 1929 with the *Chicago Daily News*. After becoming assistant sports editor of the *Chicago Daily Times*, Damata joined the *Chicago Tribune* during the late 1940s, where he remained until his retirement in 1975. He became a fixture among Chicago sportswriters.

Verdi claimed that Damata "didn't cover hockey for 45 years. He lived it. He didn't tell you how the goals were scored. He told you why. He didn't just string words together. He painted a picture. . . . He could, quite simply, write better about the sport than anyone extant because he knew better than anyone what was going on. He literally has cast aside more knowledge of the game than any of us accumulate."

As Verdi wrote in the May 24, 1988, *Chicago Tribune*: "He used to joke about how he started covering the Blackhawks as a kid himself in 1929 because nobody else wanted the job. But, until he put his last byline on a hockey story decades later, he was the only man for the job. He wrote about bad teams and mediocre teams and Stanley Cup teams and he wrote about them with passion. Ted didn't cover the Blackhawks because he had to clear the ice off his windshield in a darkened Stadium parking lot at 1 in the morning. He did it because he loved it, which is exactly how it read."

Edward Burns was another noteworthy Chicago hockey scribe during the 1920s and 1930s. A sportswriter for the *Chicago*

Tribune and a contributor to the *Sporting News*, Burns was a charter member of the National Hockey League's selection committee and is credited with originating the penalty-killing term "feathering the puck." He also influenced the NHL to expand the once thinner blue line to a width of 12 inches. ∎

game against the Reds. "It's poor policy at any time to be beaten by a minor league organization," he said in the October 19, 1937, *Chicago Daily Tribune*. "Our defense men are going to play in exhibition games exactly the way they do in the regular season—it's the best practice I know of."

More of Stewart's coaching philosophy appeared in the following day's issue. "The failure of a hocky [sic] team usually can be traced to one of two elements, failure to hustle and injuries," he said. "Last year, perhaps the Hawks were victimized by both of these handicaps. I saw the Hawks in many games which I refereed and do not believe the boys were dogging it. But some of them were discouraged and were of such temperament that they couldn't give their best. The first thing I told the team when I joined it a week ago was that I could overlook many honest mistakes but I would not tolerate refusals to hustle."

Stewart also offered his thoughts on the upcoming season. "I hope the fans won't expect us to be unbeatable," he said. "If they will be patient with our reorganization plans, I know we will give them a better show, for there is going to be less fiddling around with meaningless passes than there has been in some of the games in which the Hawks have participated in the past.

"All our work on plays has carried the thought that the fans like to see the goalie work," Stewart continued. "There won't be many silly shots the length of the rink, but whenever a man with the puck sees a chance to score he will be expected to forget the Fancy Dan passing business and take a whang at the nets.

"Though there will be much more shooting, we have not lost sight of the value of formal maneuvers," he concluded. "So far we have taken a few leaves from the book of the Cook brothers and Frank Boucher in the days when they were clicking for the New York Rangers. This great

The 1937–38 Chicago Blackhawks. (Photo courtesy of the Art Wiebe family)

trio had a number of plays and I have reason to believe that we have the players who can execute many of them."

By this time rookies Oscar "Ossie" Hanson and Cully Dahlstrom were both hustling for a center position—the only slot that Stewart had yet to fill. Their efforts must have impressed the coach because both men made the squad. The Blackhawks won their first exhibition game on October 23 against the Reds, whose roster was strengthened thanks to several Chicago players that Stewart loaned to the minor league club.

Two days later, Stewart began subjecting Johnny Gottselig and Paul Thompson to 15 minutes of penalty shot practice per day. The two veterans were designated as the team's penalty shot takers at a time when the NHL instituted a new rule allowing players to carry the puck when attempting to score, instead of taking the penalty shot from a designated position.

As training camp began to wind down, Frederic McLaughlin made an appearance in Muskegon on October 27 to assess his team's condition. Not only were the Blackhawks in top physical shape, with no injuries, they sported new red, white, and black uniforms that Stewart had designed. After winning their second exhibition game against Muskegon 6-1 on October 30, the Blackhawks returned to Chicago in good spirits, arriving early Halloween morning.

On November 1, Stewart hosted a special open house to showcase the 1937–38 Chicago Blackhawks to fans. Approximately 1,000 people attended the morning event at the Chicago Arena on Erie and McClurg Streets. Absent were Gottselig and March, who had traveled directly from Muskegon to Montreal to participate in the NHL All-Star Game. The next day, the Blackhawks held their first official practice, which was open to the public, at Chicago Stadium.

Regular Season

As Chicagoans opened their newspapers on November 4, there was no escaping the fact that hockey season had arrived. The front page of the *Chicago American* featured an action shot of rookies Cully Dahlstrom, Oscar Hanson, and Vic Heyliger spraying ice with their states. Hanson's NHL career was limited to the eight games he played for the Blackhawks in 1937–38. Heyliger, a Boston native who captained the University of Michigan hockey team the previous season, played seven games for the Blackhawks in 1937–38. After coaching at the University of Illinois from 1939–43, his NHL career included another brief stint (26 games) with Chicago in 1943–44.

Although the photo may have invoked some excitement, the accompanying article by Jim Gallagher gave the impression that the city did not have much to look forward to. "There will be few surprises for Chicago fans when the veil is rent," he wrote. "Save for a third-string center and a utility forward, the Hawks are the same team as finished in last place in the 1936–37 season. However, the boys will be dressed in nifty new uniforms. Instead of the black and buckskin Indian motif of last season, they will be appareled in outfits of black and scarlet, the most notable feature of which is black silk panties." Gallagher did, however, take note of the team's new leadership behind the bench, describing Stewart as "a little man with a big store of fire and courage."

That night, the Blackhawks began the regular season at Chicago

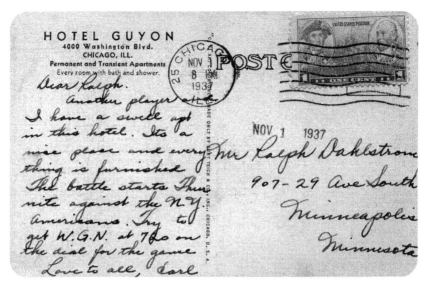

As the Blackhawks prepared for their first home game of the regular season, rookie Cully Dahlstrom sent a postcard to his brother, Ralph, in Minneapolis, encouraging the family to listen to the game on WGN radio. (Photo courtesy of the Cully Dahlstrom family)

Stadium, facing off against the New York Americans, who were led by manager Red Dutton. Chicago's starting lineup included Mike Karakas in goal, defensemen Marty Burke and Earl Seibert, and forwards Mush March, Doc Romnes, and Paul Thompson. Ticket prices ranged from $.75 to $2.50 per seat. Well-funded guests, including James Norris and James Norris, Jr., enjoyed watching the action from box seats.

The 13,000 fans in attendance (the largest crowd for a home opener in team history to date) were disappointed when the Americans beat the Blackhawks 3-0. Karakas sustained an injury during the first period that required five stitches to his forehead and the bridge of his nose. Defenseman Art Wiebe also received a few stitches during the contest.

After their rough start at home, the Blackhawks hit the road for a series of away games that required nearly 2,300 miles of travel. NHL teams mainly traveled by train during the late 1930s. "A couple of times we'd go by bus," recalled Cully Dahlstrom. "Then, we did some flying, too, depending on the time schedule. So, if we had a short schedule and wanted to get up there [to Canada] and at least get some kind of a night's rest, we'd often times fly up." In *Total Hockey: The Official Encyclo-*

Defenseman Earl Seibert and forward Mush March pose for a photo during the late 1930s. (Photo courtesy of the Boston Public Library, Leslie Jones Collection)

The Blackhawks pose for a group photo before boarding a United Airlines flight, probably during the 1940s. (Photo courtesy of the Art Wiebe family)

pedia of the National Hockey League, Don O'Hanley claimed the Detroit Red Wings were the first NHL team to travel by air during the second half of the 1938–39 season.

The Blackhawks' first away game of the season took place on November 9 against the Canadiens. Montreal's lineup included goaltender Wilf Cude, who had minded the nets for Detroit in 1934 when Chicago won its first Stanley Cup, as well as veterans like forward Aurel Joliat and defenseman Babe Siebert, the previous season's NHL MVP. The game, played before only 4,000 fans, ended in a 2-2 overtime tie.

The Blackhawks' road trip then took them to the Big Apple, where they faced off against Lester Patrick's Rangers on November 11. This time, 16,000 fans filled Madison Square Garden to watch the contest between the two American Division teams. Mush March scored an unassisted goal at 1:02 of the first period, giving Chicago the lead. Following a scoreless second period, Doc Romnes scored two goals during the third period (9:47 and 19:33). A New York goal by Cecil Dillon at 11:12

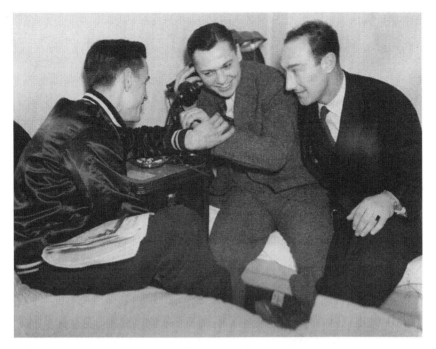

As this *New York World-Telegram* photo shows, landline phones provided plenty of entertainment for hockey players during the 1930s. Passing time at their hotel before the game, left to right, are goalie Mike Karakas and defensemen Art Wiebe and Earl Seibert. According to the *World-Telegram*, the theme song for this photo is, "Ask her if she's got a friend." (Photo courtesy of the Art Wiebe family)

was not enough to prevent the Blackhawks from registering their first win of the season.

The Blackhawks then faced off against the high-scoring Maple Leafs for two consecutive games. Only two minutes into the first game, held in Toronto, Maple Leafs sharpshooters Charlie Conacher, Harvey Jackson, and Gordon Drillon scored three times, contributing to a 7-3 Toronto victory on November 13. Back in Chicago, WGN broadcast part of the second contest following a radio address about unemployment by President Franklin Delano Roosevelt. About 13,000 fans cheered for the home team in an excitement-filled contest that ended in a 3-3 overtime tie.

Following their series against Toronto, the Blackhawks prepared for their first regular-season game against the Detroit Red Wings, who had won the Stanley Cup the previous season. At Chicago Arena, coach

Stewart subjected the team to a strenuous 90-minute drill. Joining the practice was defenseman/right wing Roger Jenkins, who had been released by the Montreal Maroons. After helping Chicago win the Stanley Cup in 1933–34, Jenkins had been traded to several teams, including the Montreal Canadiens, Boston Bruins, and Toronto Maple Leafs.

Fans were not disappointed when the Blackhawks beat Detroit on November 18, registering their first home win of the season. Following a scoreless first period, the Blackhawks came alive during the second, scoring three times in less than five minutes. On a pass from Paul Thompson, Doc Romnes scored on Detroit goalie Normie Smith, putting Chicago on the board at 13:38. Next, Thompson scored a goal of his own at 17:18, assisted by Romnes and March. Only 14 seconds later, Romnes scored the third goal of the game at 17:32, with an assist from March. Detroit's only goal came from Marty Barry at 4:10 of the third period.

After their victory over Detroit, the Blackhawks were defeated by the Bruins at home three days later, giving Boston its sixth and consecutive win of the season. The team then went on the road, losing to Detroit on November 25 and the New York Americans on November 27.

A little showmanship may have contributed to the team's 4-0 loss to the Americans. In a June 14, 1979, *San Diego Union* article, Cully Dahlstrom told writer Ben Wahrman that, in addition to skill, acting was an important part of the game. It just so happened that the Americans had a good showman in their lineup.

"You had to be in good shape and tough," Dahlstrom explained. "You had to be able to skate well and, believe it or not, you had to be a good actor—especially in the forward line trying to fake the goalie out of position. I was pretty good at that but the best in the business, in my opinion, was 'Hooley' Smith of the New York Americans. He'd drop his shoulder, draw his face into a determined look, fake the shot, and then quickly move a few feet to the right or left and blaze the puck past the frustrated goalie who had moved out to block that feint."

By this time, the Blackhawks had faced most of their opponents at least once, except for the Montreal Maroons, who had defeated them in all six matchups the previous season. Chicago's losing trend against the Maroons continued on November 30 with a 1-0 loss. With just two wins, the Blackhawks' performance improved in December, the best month

Earl Seibert (left) and Cully Dahlstrom (right) enjoy Chicago's winter weather.
(Photo courtesy of the Art Wiebe family)

---

of the regular season. During the first half of the month the team won three of its first four games, beginning with a 2-1 victory over the New York Rangers on December 2.

The December 11, 1937, *Detroit Free Press* shed light on the caliber of player the team had in rookie Cully Dahlstrom, who had quickly become "the darling of Chicago puck crowds." Dahlstrom had kept quiet about an injured jaw, opting for a liquid diet when eating became too painful. After playing two games with what ultimately turned out to be a broken jaw, he refused to sit on the bench. The Blackhawks outfitted Dahlstrom with a specially designed aluminum brace, lined with sponge rubber, to keep his jaw intact when he was on the ice.

Brothers Cecil "Tiny" and Paul Thompson. (Photo courtesy of the Boston Public Library, Leslie Jones Collection)

On December 21, the Blackhawks played the first of three road games around the Christmas holiday. During a contest against the Boston Bruins, Paul Thompson became the first player in NHL history to score a goal against his own brother, Cecil "Tiny" Thompson. Although Boston won the game 2-1, Chicago recorded a 3-1 victory over the New York Rangers on December 26. The Blackhawks finished the 1937 calendar year with a 2-2 overtime tie with the Red Wings on December 30. That game marked the beginning of a disappointing 10-game stretch in which the team recorded just one victory.

As the New Year began, the Blackhawks welcomed another American-born player to the team when Virgil Johnson was acquired from the

AHA's St. Paul Saints on January 8. At the time, Minnesota sportswriter Perry Dotson wrote: "It will be a long time, if ever, before the St. Paul hockey club has on its roster again two such fine athletic competitors as Virg Johnson, defense star who has just been sold to the Chicago Blackhawks, and Cully Dahlstrom, ace center who was drafted from the Saints this fall.

"Whenever the victory road was rough for St. Paul's advance, it was either Virg or Cully who continued to play his best game and pull the team out of trouble," Dotson continued. "Time and again they delivered in the pinch because neither knew what it was to quit in the face of big odds or discouragement."

Although Johnson remained with the team through the end of the season, he would return to the minor leagues for five years before rejoining the Blackhawks again in 1943–44. Dahlstrom remained on the Blackhawks' roster through 1945. By this point in the season, *Chicago American* sportswriter Jim Gallagher called him "a great prospect," noting that he was "rated one of the prize rookies of the year" and "certainly is the best prospect the Hawks have signed since they bought the ill-fated Jack Leswick a few years ago."

In a January 6, 1938, article, Gallagher explained that Dahlstrom initially went pro with the Minneapolis Millers, who paid him a weekly salary of $25, because it was better than any other opportunity available to him during the Great Depression. Regarding the job as a "stopgap," Dahlstrom had planned on quitting hockey when full-time work became available at the Minneapolis-Moline Farm Implement Company, where he worked during the summer.

After cracking into the big leagues, the Blackhawks gave Dahlstrom a reason to leave his skates on, but the promotion had not gone to his head. "I'm not a speed demon on skates," he told Gallagher. "But you have to skate faster up here, so I'm going to skate faster. I just have to."

In addition to skating faster, Bill Stewart noticed that Dahlstrom also had improved in other areas of the game. "He had a habit of keeping his head down, watching the puck, which made it easy to hit him," he said. "We've cured him of that, however, and the way he skates now reminds me of Doc Romnes."

Stewart also described other attributes that Dahlstrom brought to the team. "'Cully' has long legs, long arms and uses a long stick," he added. "That combination makes it awfully hard for a defense man to check him when he comes in on a play. If the defense man goes for the puck, Dahlstrom can push it through and slip around him; if he goes for Dahlstrom, the puck is free for a pass."

After losing the first two games of the New Year at home to the Canadiens and Rangers, the Blackhawks pleased fans at Chicago Stadium by beating the Montreal Maroons 1-0 on January 9. The team then recorded three consecutive overtime ties on the road against the Americans, Canadiens, and Maple Leafs. After a punishing 7-2 home loss to the Maple Leafs on January 16, the Blackhawks were beaten on the road twice more, falling to the Bruins on January 18 and the Red Wings on January 20. Facing those same opponents, the team seemed to come alive with a pair of home victories, beating the Bruins on January 23 and the Red Wings on January 27. The Blackhawks ended the month with a tie against the Rangers on January 30.

February was the most difficult month of the regular season for the Blackhawks. The team's only victories happened on the road: a 2-1 win over the Maple Leafs on February 12 and a 6-5 win against the Maroons on February 22. However, the latter game signified an awakening for the team.

The Blackhawks began the month of March with three consecutive home wins. After defeating the Bruins on March 3, Chicago pummeled the Maroons 7-1 on March 6. The team then played its final home game of the regular season against the Montreal Canadiens, winning 4-1 on March 10. Though some were skeptical of their ability to make the playoffs, the lackluster Blackhawks still had a fighting chance. Helping matters was forward Paul Thompson, who ranked as the American Division's top individual scorer.

After hitting the road for the final three games of the regular season, things did not go well. On March 13, the Red Wings beat the Blackhawks 5-1. Late in the first period, Detroit forward Carl Liscombe scored three goals in only 1 minute and 52 seconds.

Although the New York Americans beat them 2-1 two days later, the Blackhawks made the playoffs when the Red Wings (their challengers for third place in the American division) lost to the Montreal

CHICAGO STADIUM TICKET PRICES

During the late 1930s, fans interested in season tickets could purchase a 24-game Chicago Stadium box seat for $60 (about $1,113 in 2021). Seats in the first 10 rows of the mezzanine cost $42 ($779), while all other mezzanine seats and arena seats cost $36 ($668). First balcony seats could be had for $30 ($557). Fans not interested in paying for an entire season had the option of buying tickets for three games in advance. Single tickets ranged in price from $.75 ($13.91) to $2.50 ($46.38). By comparison, new men's dress shirts could be purchased for less than $2 ($37), and dress hats cost about $3 ($56). ∎

Canadiens. With a playoff appearance assured, the Blackhawks faced off against the league-leading Boston Bruins, who some favored as the season's likely Stanley Cup winner. To avoid the prospect of injuries, both teams played a safe, wide open game on March 20, which Boston won 6-1.

During the regular season, the Blackhawks had won only 14 games in 20 weeks of regular play. However, Stewart had made the most of the talent on Chicago's bench. "Realizing he had no individual stars and little bench strength, he built a strategy around tightly integrated team play," wrote Herm Weiskopf in the March 28, 1960, issue of *Sports Illustrated*. "To compensate for his squad's lack of depth, Stewart became a quick-change artist, installing and withdrawing entire five-man units after just two or three minutes' play. This maneuver was as successful as it was novel, for it helped keep the players fresh and enabled Stewart to develop two good offensive lines. This didn't show up in the Black Hawks' regular-season record, for the 1937–38 team didn't win any more games than the hopeless 1936–37 team. However, by Stanley Cup time, Bill Stewart's hard work and sound strategy began to show results."

As the Blackhawks prepared to face the Montreal Canadiens and the New York Rangers got ready for a matchup against the New York Americans, George Strickler offered his observation on the playoffs in

Left to Right: Mike Karakas, Alex Levinsky, Doc Romnes, Johnny Gottselig, coach Bill Stewart, Earl Seibert, Paul Thompson, and Mush March celebrate securing a playoff berth in March 1938. (Le Studio du Hockey/Hockey Hall of Fame)

Members of the 1937–38 Chicago Blackhawks pose for a photo with coach Bill Stewart. (Photo courtesy of the Boston Public Library, Leslie Jones Collection)

the March 22, 1938, *Chicago Daily Tribune*, writing: "Only in hocky [sic] is it possible for a team to finish sixth in a season's pennant race [and] then go on to become champion of the universe and, what is more re- markable, be accepted as the rightful ruler."

CHAPTER 8

Cinderella Story

---

n George Vass's book, *The Chicago Black Hawks Story*, defenseman Alex Levinsky described the overall vibe as the Blackhawks prepared for the first round of postseason competition. "We were so bad that I thought we'd be eliminated in our first playoff series by the Canadiens," he said. "So I packed all my clothes in my car and sent my wife home to Toronto."

Alex Levinsky (left) and Doc Romnes (right) with a friend (unidentified). (Photo courtesy of the Doc Romnes family)

Against the light and fast Canadiens, the Blackhawks used heavy bodychecking to upset their timing. During the series' first game, played at the Montreal Forum and officiated by Cecil "Babe" Dye (one of the original 1926 Blackhawks) and future NHL President Clarence Campbell, Chicago drew first blood when Paul Thompson scored at 1:31 of the first period. Montreal captain Babe Siebert responded with a goal at 10:58. Chicago was the first to score during the second period when Mush March put the puck past goaltender Wilf Cude at 12:23, but the back-and-forth action continued as Montreal's Toe Blake scored on Karakas at 13:38. Another Montreal goal followed at 13:45 when Clifford "Red" Goupille managed to elude the entire Chicago team and put one past Karakas.

During the third period, Johnny Gottselig tied things up for the Blackhawks with a goal at 9:30. The formidable Toe Blake then managed to slip another goal past Karakas at 11:32. Chicago rookie Cully Dahlstrom answered for the Blackhawks seconds later, tying up the game once again at 11:51, but Toe Blake registered a hat trick by scoring for a third time at 17:32. A little over one minute later, Goupille scored his second goal of the game, and the Habs beat the Blackhawks 6-4.

During the opening game, Carl Voss injured his knee and was replaced by Harold Jackson, who had rejoined the Chicago lineup after recovering from a broken collarbone. Following the loss, Bill Stewart and the Blackhawks returned to Chicago with their backs against the wall. Levinsky may have figured he would be back home in Toronto in just a few days, considering the team needed to win the next two matches in the best-of-three series to advance to the semifinals.

Although the Blackhawks were optimistic, the odds were against them. They had played the Canadiens seven times since the beginning of the season, winning once and tying two games. However, Chicago had offensive power in Paul Thompson, who ended the regular season with 22 goals and 44 points (third best in the NHL). Montreal had a scoring machine of its own in fourth-ranked Georges Mantha (23 goals, 42 points).

In the second game against Montreal, the Blackhawks delivered a stunning performance that befuddled sportswriters and many fans. After a slow start, the game got interesting after about 10 minutes when

Mush March prepares to recover the puck from goaltender Mike Karakas in Chicago's first playoff game against the Canadiens at the Montreal Forum on March 22, 1938. (Conrad Poirier, Bibliothèque et Archives nationales du Québec)

Cully Dahlstrom sustained a cut on his scalp. After Chicago argued (unsuccessfully) for a Montreal penalty, the game resumed with emotions running high. Canadiens forward Joffre Desilets instigated a fight with Johnny Gottselig. When the smoke cleared, Desilets was handed a major penalty, while Gottselig received a double minor. The momentum shifted in Chicago's favor when defenseman Earl Seibert put his team on the board at 17:58 of the first period.

Seibert scored another goal for the Blackhawks at 10:06 of the third period. After stealing the puck, Gottselig expertly wove his way through a crowd of Montreal players and increased the Blackhawks' lead with another goal at 13:34. Finally, Paul Thompson scored a fourth goal for the Blackhawks with only one second remaining in the third period.

"Earl Seibert, Johnny Gottselig, and Goalie Mike Karakas lifted the Hawks to championship heights," wrote George Strickler in the March 26, 1938, *Chicago Daily Tribune*. "Karakas's performance was as surprising as it was impressive. Seibert and Gottselig performed with their customary brilliance, but Karakas, who had seen six Canadien goals fly past him in Montreal Tuesday night, brought new hope to Hawk followers as he turned away thrust after thrust in the first and second periods when a goal would have tied the score and possibly altered the entire aspect of the game."

With the series tied, Chicago and Montreal proceeded to a third, win-or-die match at the Forum. The 11,375 fans in attendance witnessed vicious bodychecking from both sides as the two teams took out their frustrations on one another. During the first five minutes of the game, Mush March and Toe Blake nearly squared off twice, but no fights erupted. Gottselig was the first to score for Chicago with a backhand shot at 18:24 of the first period, but Montreal's Johnny "Black Cat" Gagnon tied the game at 8:52 of the second period.

The Habs pulled ahead briefly during the third period when Gottselig accidentally put the puck in the Chicago net while trying to clear the rebound on a shot from Georges Mantha at 12:46. Mush March and Toe Blake nearly dropped the gloves again but managed to avoid an entanglement. Although it appeared that Chicago would be eliminated, defenseman Earl Seibert kept his team in the Stanley Cup playoffs.

After receiving a pass from Gottselig, Seibert tied the game at 18:34, sending the contest into overtime. As the extra period of play began, both teams contended with an added variable when heavy fog developed over the ice. Paul Thompson ultimately scored a game-winning breakaway goal for Chicago at 11:49, after receiving a pass from Louis Trudel.

After defeating the Canadiens, the Blackhawks advanced to the semifinals, where they prepared to meet the New York Americans at Madison Square Garden. The Americans had just bested the New York Rangers in their quarterfinals series. During the regular season, the Blackhawks had failed to win any games against the Americans. Two of Chicago's star players received a morale boost on March 28 when Paul Thompson (First Team) and Earl Seibert (Second Team) received All-Star honors.

Against the Americans, Stewart changed his strategy, directing his players to fire low on goaltender Earl Robertson, whose weakness was stopping low shots. The series' opening game began well for Chicago when Carl Voss scored at 5:19 of the first period. During the early part of the second period, New York's Allan Murray bodychecked Mike Karakas

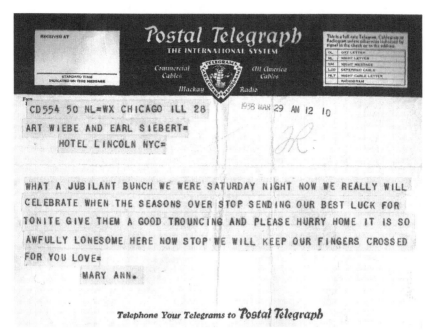

Mary Ann Wiebe sent a congratulatory telegram to husband Art Wiebe and defenseman Earl Seibert when the Blackhawks advanced in the playoffs. (Photo courtesy of the Art Wiebe family)

into the Chicago goalpost, opening a gash in his scalp that required three stitches to close. Although Stewart demanded that a penalty be called on Murray, referee Mickey Ion said Karakas had held the puck outside the crease.

After a 27-minute game delay, momentum shifted in favor of the Americans, who put five forwards on the ice. New York's Nels "Old Poison" Stewart scored on Karakas at 16:47 of the second period. Then, Johnny "Long Shot" Sorrell scored a critical game-winning goal for the Americans at 15:52 of the third period. A holding penalty against Paul Thompson resulted in a penalty shot for New York's Lorne Carr late in the third period, which was blocked by Karakas.

Dave "Sweeney" Schriner scored an insurance goal for New York at 19:08 of the third period. Karakas, still stinging from the scalp injury, was knocked out cold when Schriner careened into the Chicago cage. Although the battered netminder returned to the game after a time-out was called, the Blackhawks failed to rebound. The sobering 3-1 loss put Chicago only one game away from elimination in the best-of-three series.

Chicago and New York faced off again on April 1 at Chicago Stadium. Before the action started, Cully Dahlstrom learned that he had received the Frank Calder Trophy as the NHL's top rookie. The Blackhawks dominated the game, immediately putting strong pressure on the Americans. During the first six minutes, goalie Earl Robertson stopped Chicago from scoring seven times.

After 17 minutes of play, Chicago's Jack Shill fell in the middle of the rink with New York's Joe Jerwa, who kicked at Shill twice. Officials intervened as Shill and Jerwa prepared to drop the gloves. "A dispute arose over the penalty, finally reaching the riot stage in front of the Hawk bench, where Jerwa sassed Manager Bill Stewart and was promptly promised a thorough whipping," wrote George Strickler in the April 1, 1938, *Chicago Daily Tribune*. "Little Bill tore off his overcoat and started for the husky American, but was restrained. When Jerwa made another remark Stewart again started for him. The officials persuaded Stewart to don his coat and sentenced Shill and Jerwa to the penalty box on minors."

Chicago put intense pressure on Robertson during the second period but failed to score despite power-play opportunities. During the third period, the Americans stepped up their efforts. When Dahlstrom was penalized for tripping New York forward Thomas "Cowboy" Anderson at the eight-minute mark, Nels Stewart scored on Karakas, but officials disallowed the goal because of interference from forward Eddie Wiseman.

The Blackhawks' fate hung in the balance as the game proceeded through a scoreless first overtime period. A second overtime round began with an exciting breakaway that pitted Earl Seibert against the entire New York team. However, the "Flying Dutchman" failed to score on Robertson.

Then, at 12:33 a.m., Dahlstrom affirmed his Calder Trophy nomination by scoring the game-winning goal 13 minutes into the period. "The slender wing took a long pass from Louis Trudel, who had broken away down the left side, and hammered it high into the corner of the net over the outstretched arm of goalie Earl Robertson," wrote Strickler, comparing Robertson's performance during the second game to that of the late Charlie Gardiner, but describing Karakas as having "shaky moments."

Dahlstrom's critical goal kept Chicago's dream of advancing to the Stanley Cup finals alive. After the Blackhawks defeated New York in game two, the series shifted back to the Big Apple. From there, the winning team would travel immediately to Toronto and face the Canadian Division champion Maple Leafs in the finals. Toronto had won its best-of-five semifinals series against the American Division champion Boston Bruins, steamrolling them in three straight games despite beating them only once during six regular-season matchups.

More than 15,500 fans packed into Madison Square Garden, hopeful that the Americans would eliminate the Blackhawks. The crowd was elated when Lorne Carr scored on Chicago with a 50-foot shot from center ice at 19:40 of the first period. Carr's goal was scored on the power play, after Jack Shill was penalized for tripping New York's Johnny Gallagher. Chicago responded with strong efforts from March and Thompson, both of whom nearly scored on Robertson.

Like the previous contest, game three was not without drama. During the first period, Gottselig went down behind the Chicago goal at the hands of Gallagher. His nose bleeding, Gottselig demanded a penalty, resulting in an explosive argument with referee Ag Smith. Earl Seibert finally tied the game at 14:43 of the second period. Alex Levinsky scored another goal for the Blackhawks nearly two minutes later, which was challenged by the Americans, who claimed that the goal judge's light had not gone on. When it was discovered that two fans had restrained the judge, the goal was allowed, and Chicago pulled ahead 2-1.

The Blackhawks scored again at 15:53 of the third period, with a goal from Doc Romnes. Although Red Beattie answered for the Americans at 16:29, making it a 3-2 game, New York was unable to score again. To the astonishment of many, the Blackhawks had advanced to the Stanley Cup finals.

Filling in for *Chicago Times* Sports Editor Marvin McCarthy, Bill Stewart shared his thoughts on the team's unexpected advancement in the playoffs, commenting: "Many a hockey fan is pinching himself and wondering if these are the same Black Hawks he saw earlier this season. And to tell you the truth, the whole truth and nothing but the truth, so am I! Shooting straight from the shoulder, I must admit that when I first took over management of the Hawks this season I had little hope of qualifying for the Stanley Cup series. . . .

"How have the boys done it? The answer to that, in as few words as possible, is 'spirit.' This is the goldangest bunch of fellows you ever saw. Now I'm not kidding myself or Chicago's hockey fans by saying that they are a great bunch of players. They're not. They recognize their own weaknesses and any expert in the game will tell you that there are a number of big-league squads with greater physical possibilities. So much is true.

"But these Hawks simply won't admit defeat. They've made up for lack of personnel with an overdose of will to win. They've got as fine a competitive spirit as any team I've ever seen in all the years—please don't ask me how many—I've been connected with sports. They're greatest in the clutch, and show their real ability when they have to come from behind.

"Did I mention 'come from behind'? It seems that's what we have been doing ever since the start of the season. We had to rally even to qualify for the Stanley Cup series. We had to rally to beat the Montreal Canadiens in our first playoff series. Then we lose the first game in Montreal? That meant we had to beat the Canadiens the next two in order to get into the semifinal-round. We had that very same problem after losing the first game of our present series to the Americans in New York, only more so. Here was a team we hadn't whipped all season—and all we had to do was beat them two straight! Thank gosh, we eased the situation considerably by winning last night. That competitive spirit, which flares anew whenever the team has its back to the wall, will have to carry through again Sunday night. I'm not making any predictions— never have and never intend to—but fighting spirit goes a long way in settling these battles."

In the same article, Stewart commented on the goal that allowed the team to advance in the playoffs: "I must say a few words about our prize youngster, Cully Dahlstrom," he wrote. "Early yesterday, he was informed that he had won the Frank Calder Rookie Cup—awarded annually to the most promising rookie in the league. Naturally, he was feeling great. Just before we started the final overtime period last night,

Left to Right: Syl Apps, Conn Smythe, head coach Dick Irvin, and Gordon Drillon in 1938. (Photo courtesy of the Boston Public Library, Leslie Jones Collection)

I patted him on the back and said, 'Cully, make this your perfect day. You already have that trophy. Now go out and get this goal.' He did. Can any manager ask for more?"

Following their victory over the Americans, the Blackhawks faced the Maple Leafs for a best-of-five series. While Toronto's players had been able to rest for a week before the finals began, the Blackhawks had been traveling extensively and skating hard. Chicago entered the finals round with several Stanley Cup veterans. Paul Thompson, Doc Romnes, Mush March, Louis Trudel, Roger Jenkins, and Johnny Gottselig had all been with the team for its first Stanley Cup victory in 1933–34. They faced off against a Toronto team, led by coach Dick Irvin and owner Conn Smythe, which included scoring aces Gordon Drillon and Sylvanus "Syl" Apps, and enforcer Reginald "Red" Horner. Drillon (26 goals, 52 points) and Apps (21 goals, 50 points) were the league's top two scorers in 1937–38.

Constantine Falkland Cary "Conn" Smythe

Widely recognized as one of professional hockey's most colorful and influential figures, Conn Smythe was born on February 1, 1895, in Toronto. He owned the Toronto Maple Leafs for 34 years. As Tim Burke wrote in the November 20, 1980, issue of Montreal's *Gazette*, Smythe and his team were synonymous: "In Conn Smythe's heyday, the Maple Leafs were molded in the image of their stormy and colorful owner—tough, tenacious and Union Jack."

Before becoming an NHL icon, Smythe was captain of the University of Toronto's Varsity Blues hockey team. After earning an engineering degree, he served in both World War I and World War II and was a prisoner of war for 15 months during the first conflict, after being captured by the Germans. After helping to build the New York Rangers, in February 1927 Smythe spent $10,000 to buy the Toronto St. Patricks, which he renamed the Maple Leafs, and was instrumental in the construction of Maple Leaf Gardens, where the team would play for many years.

Frank Selke, Sr., served as Smythe's assistant general manager for two decades until becoming the Montreal Canadiens' general manager. Selke's move to Montreal inflamed a relationship between the two men that already had soured. Nevertheless, Selke's respect for Smythe remained intact. "He was a difficult but wonderful fellow," Selke recalled in the same issue of the *Gazette*. "It was he more than anyone else who brought the NHL from a horse-and-buggy circuit to major-league status."

Smythe was something of a paradox. Selke explained that during his first six months in Toronto, Smythe paid his wages from his own salary, but that there were other occasions "when I could have hit him over the head with a baseball bat, and enjoyed it. It was strange how such a wonderful fellow could do such crazy things now and then. But his good points far and away outweighed his bad ones."

"He was quite a character," said the late Tom Gaston, a longtime Hockey Hall of Fame volunteer who met Smythe. "If he shook hands with you, that was his bond. He might've had his faults, but if he shook hands on a deal, he never reneged. A handshake was his honor."

Under Smythe, Toronto had one of the greatest dynasties in professional hockey, winning the Stanley Cup seven times between 1932 and 1951. In 1961, he sold his ownership stake in the Maple Leafs to a group that included his son, Stafford Smythe. That year, he was instrumental in the 1961 construction of the Hockey Hall of Fame building. Smythe was inducted into the Hockey Hall of Fame in 1958, the Ontario Sports Hall of Fame in 1966, and Canada's Sports Hall of Fame in 1977. He died on November 18, 1980, at age 85.

Gordon Arthur "Gordie" Drillon

Born in Moncton, New Brunswick, on October 23, 1913, Gordie Drillon was an offensive force for the Maple Leafs during the 1930s. The 6'2", 178-pound winger was nearly named rookie of the year in 1936–37, but the honor went to teammate Syl Apps, with whom he played on the DAD Line with Bob Davidson. In 1938, Drillon was the NHL's top scorer and received the Lady Byng trophy for gentlemanly play.

Drillon, who helped pioneer the practice of deflection by camping out near the opposition's goal to capitalize on tip-in shots, spent all but one of his seven NHL seasons in Toronto, ending his career with Montreal in 1942-43. In all, he racked up 294 points (155 goals and 139 assists) in 311 NHL games. During his career, Drillon received All-Star honors three times, including 1941–42, when he helped the Maple Leafs win the Stanley Cup.

Drillon was inducted into the Hockey Hall of Fame in 1975. He died on September 23, 1986, in St. John, New Brunswick. Three years later, Drillon was honored again when he was posthumously inducted into Canada's Sports Hall of Fame.

Charles Joseph Sylvanus (Syl) Apps

When he signed with the Toronto Maple Leafs in 1936, Syl Apps ranked among the best amateur hockey players in Ontario. Born in Paris, Ontario, on January 18, 1915, the McMaster University student also was a two-time Canadian champion pole-vaulter, ranking as British Empire champion in 1934 and placing sixth at the 1936 Summer Olympics in Berlin. Quiet and modest, Apps was an exceptionally clean player. In the

March 3, 1971, *Ottawa Citizen*, Jim Coleman said he "was the pre-eminent stylist among professional hockey's centremen. He was big, handsome and he skated with extraordinary grace and speed."

After leading the Maple Leafs in scoring, Apps became the team's first player to win the Calder Trophy as rookie of the year. Throughout most of his 10-season career, he was team captain in Toronto, playing on three Stanley Cup-winning teams (1942, 1947, and 1948), receiving All-Star honors five times, and winning the Lady Byng trophy for gentlemanly play in 1942. During his career, Apps scored 432 points (201 goals and 231 assists) in 423 regular-season games.

Apps was inducted into the Hockey Hall of Fame in 1961. After hockey, he pursued a career in politics, becoming Ontario Athletic Commissioner in 1946 and serving as a Conservative member of Parliament from 1963–74. Apps was inducted into Canada's Sports Hall of Fame in 1975. Two years later, he was named to the Order of Canada and inducted into the Ontario Sports Hall of Fame. Apps died on Christmas Eve in 1998, at age 83.

George Reginald "Red" Horner

Red Horner was a longtime fixture in Toronto's hockey scene. After playing junior for the OHA's Toronto Marlboros, the red-haired Horner went pro with the Toronto Maple Leafs in 1928 and remained with the team until 1940. A native of Lynden, Ontario, he quickly became a fan favorite as one of the league's hardest-hitting defensemen.

As Toronto's enforcer, Horner was a physical threat to the Blackhawks. However, he also could score goals. During the 1937–38 regular season, Horner racked up 24 points (four goals and 20 assists), making him the leading point-maker among NHL defensemen.

During his 12-season career, Horner amassed 1,264 penalty minutes during 490 regular-season games—an NHL record at the time of his retirement in 1940. After hockey, he became a fuel salesman. When Horner died in 2005 at age 95, he was the oldest living former NHL player and the oldest living Hockey Hall of Fame member.

Stanley Cup Finals

The Blackhawks arrived in Toronto the morning of Monday, April 4, with plenty of time to spare before the following day's sold-out game. The team appeared to be healthy overall. Mush March was nursing a sore hip, which he had bruised badly, and Louis Trudel was contending with a charley horse. Mike Karakas, who had blocked a shot with his right foot in the team's last game against the Americans, had a sore toe, which prevented him from putting on his shoe as the train pulled into Toronto.

"He had to limp to a taxicab in his stocking feet, and through the hotel lobby toting one shoe," explained a December 10, 1938, *Collier's* article. "When the swelling failed to go down late that afternoon, Mike began to wonder if it would bother his goaltending. When the light blue color of the swelling blended into a purple, he called a club physician and learned that he had suffered a broken toe sometime during that last game in New York."

Karakas was no stranger to playing through injuries. "My dad played his entire career without a mask," recalls his daughter, Joan Karakas, who says her "ruggedly handsome" dad's face had taken more than 500 stitches by the end of his career. "Knowing my father, if something happened he would be the type to go back out and play," she said. "Even in his normal life, he didn't fall apart when something happened; he just kept going. He was not a crybaby; he just sucked it up and did what he had to do."

Nevertheless, the following day Karakas was scratched from the roster and Chicago was without a goaltender. Stewart and Bill Tobin began searching for a replacement and named the New York Rangers' Dave Kerr as their first choice. In a March 25, 1962, *Chicago Tribune Magazine* article, Ted Damata explained: "Kerr was willing, and so was the coach, manager, and head of the Toronto organization—one Connie Smythe, who from a Chicago viewpoint, tied Reginald [Red] Horner as the No. 1 villain of the series. Smythe pointed out that Frank Calder, the league president, would have to give his approval—a mere formality."

Based on Damata's version of the story, Stewart and Tobin believed their goaltending quagmire had been solved. However, Calder decided that Kerr "was valued property of the Rangers and could not be exposed to injury." At 6 p.m., a phone call from the league office was received in the bar of the Toronto hotel where the Blackhawks were staying. Seated there was Alfred Ernest "English Alfie" Moore, a minor-league goalie with the IAHL's Pittsburgh Hornets, who learned that he would be Chicago's backup goaltender that night. However, the same message was not immediately relayed to the Blackhawks.

Moore's experience consisted of 18 NHL games with the New York Americans the previous season and playing for a multitude of minor-league teams since his 1926–27 debut with the AHA's Chicago Cardinals. While some historians claim Moore was not intoxicated, Damata noted that he began consuming bourbon in the hotel bar during the late morning hours, while waiting for a chance to score game tickets from Tobin. Moore eventually connected with Tobin in the afternoon and then returned to the bar for more drinking.

"The call almost sobered Moore, but not quite," Damata wrote. "It was the first the Hawks had heard that Moore, not Kerr, would be in their nets." In the April 7, 1938, *Chicago Daily Tribune*, sportswriter George Strickler claimed the Maple Leafs kept Moore "away from the Chicagoans until Stewart and business manager Bill Tobin forced a showdown a few minutes before the game."

Johnny Gottselig described how and where the Blackhawks eventually found Moore and escorted him to Maple Leaf Gardens. "Alfie had been a pretty good goalie for Pittsburgh and I had gotten to know him from the times we had trained there," he explained in an April 1979 *Hockey* article. "So they sent me out to find him."

Moore's wife told Gottselig that Alfie could be found in a neighborhood tavern, so by this time he apparently had moved on from the hotel bar. More barhopping ensued; Gottselig explained that he was too late in arriving at the neighborhood tavern, but eventually caught up with the inebriated Moore at another watering hole. "He and his buddies were going pretty strong when I got there," Gottselig said. "When Alf saw me walk in, he shouted, 'John, am I glad to see you! Got any tickets for the game tonight?' 'Alf,' I said, 'you're going to have the best seat in the house.'"

Moore apparently did not get tickets from Tobin earlier that afternoon, or plan to suit up for Chicago after receiving the NHL's call, if events transpired as Damata described. Against his will, Moore reported to Maple Leaf Gardens an hour before game time. Still drunk and fearful of putting the Blackhawks in an even more difficult situation, he learned that Frank Calder and Conn Smythe had not yet learned of his presence in the arena. Knowing this, Moore initially refused to dress for the game.

According to Bill Stewart III, his grandfather and Moore were on the same page. "They brought him in the room and, right away, my grandfather said, 'No way, I'll play goal!' Of course, the guys wouldn't have any part of that, so they put him in the shower and fed him some coffee to try and sober him up." In his article, Damata confirmed: "Gottselig and Paul Thompson held him under a cold shower. Trainer Eddie Froelich rubbed him down while players poured black coffee into him."

As the Blackhawks attended to him, Moore's anger with the Maple Leafs began to build. "While trainers rubbed him down and took other measures calculated to restore his equilibrium, Moore vented his ire on Smythe and the Leafs, who had placed him in an embarrassing position," wrote Strickler in the April 6, 1938, *Chicago Daily Tribune*.

Recalling the incident in the same day's *Boston Globe*, Moore said: "They [the Blackhawks] didn't even know I was to play. Kerr was getting dressed. Right then I knew I had been made the sucker. I was so mad that when Smythe poked his head into the door I told him 'I hope I stop every puck you fellows fire even if I have to eat the rubber.'"

Stewart, whose blood boiled hotter than Moore's, set out to find Smythe and Calder. While accounts of what happened next vary slightly from source to source, one thing is clear: fists began to fly.

Bill Stewart's grandson, Paul Stewart, once explained: "Smythe sent word over to my grandfather that there was no way [he could use Kerr], and why didn't he suit up like Lester Patrick had done a few years previously. My grandfather took it as a personal insult. He went ripping out of the room after him, and they got into it."

Bill Stewart III added: "There were some blows thrown. It wasn't a paper deal; they went after each other. Of course, he went right in the office. So they picked him up, then they literally threw him out, because he was going to kill Smythe."

Although Damata claimed that Calder, not Smythe, opposed Chicago's use of Kerr, other sources suggest Toronto's boss had no intention of allowing the Rangers' netminder to play for the Blackhawks. The December 10, 1938, issue of *Collier's* said that "Smythe doubted out loud that the Karakas big toe was broken at all; said it was just a Yankee trick to get a good Canadian goalie."

Toronto Globe and Mail Sports Editor Tommy Munns recounted Smythe telling Stewart: "You can use Karakas, of course, or you can have the choice of using Alfie Moore, but I won't go for your idea of bringing in Kerr, a star from another National League team." Munns said Stewart initially refused to use Moore, indicating that he would use Karakas if Kerr was not an option, prompting Smythe to remark: "That proves my point. You say you'll use Karakas—then you admit he is able to play."

In his account of the skirmish, Damata confirmed that Stewart went to Smythe's office to protest the use of Moore and described how "in the heat of the argument, Stewart called Smythe a liar. . . . Smythe and Hal Cotton, a former Toronto player, and others won the argument from Stewart with flying fists and then shoved him bodily out of the office."

Munns said the fighting occurred outside the dressing room, "with both doing some hefty swinging." Ultimately, police intervened to break up the fisticuffs. Stewart emerged with bruises on his head and a cut over one eye. After the scrum, Munns claimed that Smythe said: "The Hawks are the only team in the league who haven't their own farm and their own goaltender. If they weren't so cheap they wouldn't be in this jam."

In the April 7, 1938, *Chicago Daily Tribune*, George Strickler said the fight between Stewart and Smythe had more to do with Toronto's handling of the situation than it did with the selection of Moore. Following the first game, Stewart had indicated that, after Kerr, Moore had been his next choice for a backup. However, it was Toronto's secretive handling of the matter that led to the brawl.

Beyond Kerr, other factors likely contributed to the intensity of Stewart and Smythe's entanglement. "There weren't too many Americans in the league back in those days," Paul Stewart explained. "There has always been that provincial attitude, and Smythe was probably the most provincial of them all."

According to Munns, at Stewart's request Bill Tobin gathered Chicago reporters so the coach could explain what happened from his viewpoint, followed by a "bitter, forceful managerial peptalk, exhorting the players, who finally left the dressing-room in a fighting pitch."

In the same *Hockey* article, Gottselig recalled how Stewart, enraged after his fisticuffs with Smythe, stormed back into the Blackhawks' dressing room before the game, explaining: "He picked up a hammer and started pounding, shouting at us, 'See what they did to me! Go pound them!'"

Dramatizing the moment, Damata said Stewart came "charging thru the clubhouse door like an angry, wounded bull. He was bleeding from a cut eye, his face battered and bruised, and from between swollen lips an angry Scottish burr overcame the hard, clipped Boston accent and filled the air with blue smoke for yards around." When the Blackhawks and Maple Leafs encountered each other in the corridor, Gottselig remembered sticks flying.

Stewart's fireworks did not end with Smythe and Cotton. "Before the game, wild with rage, he was in the promenade in front of the box seats and behind the players' bench fighting with King Clancy," Munns wrote. "They didn't exactly come to blows, but they did plenty of hefty jostling."

In another article, Munns explained that the Maple Leafs began their pregame warm-up at 8:20 p.m. With only two minutes remaining until the puck drop, the Blackhawks had not yet appeared on the ice. They finally emerged less than one minute before the action began.

"Most of the crowd had arrived by this time; photographers were getting ready to shoot, while up in a blue section was perched a lens trained on the ice like a small machine-gun," Munns wrote. "Appearance of Mickey Ion and Johnny Mitchell on the ice settled another important question. There had been no pre-game announcement as to which officials would work tonight's game. They must have received quite a shock. There hardly was a boo when they were introduced."

Alfie Moore's brother, a former goaltender named Lawrence (Laurie), was in the stands. When he learned that his big brother would be in goal for Chicago, Laurie supposedly was overcome with a sick feeling, forcing him to step outside for air.

In the series with Toronto, Stewart adjusted his strategy to empha-

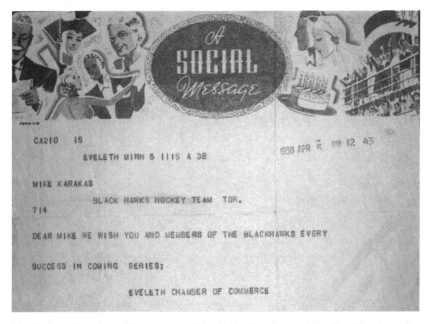

CA210   15

EVELETH MINN 5 1115 A 38

1938 APR 5 PM 12 45

MIKE KARAKAS

BLACK HAWKS HOCKEY TEAM TOR.

714

DEAR MIKE WE WISH YOU AND MEMBERS OF THE BLACKHAWKS EVERY

SUCCESS IN COMING SERIES:

EVELETH CHAMBER OF COMMERCE

The Eveleth Chamber of Commerce wished Mike Karakas and the Blackhawks well as they faced off against the Maple Leafs in game one. (Photo courtesy of the Mike Karakas family)

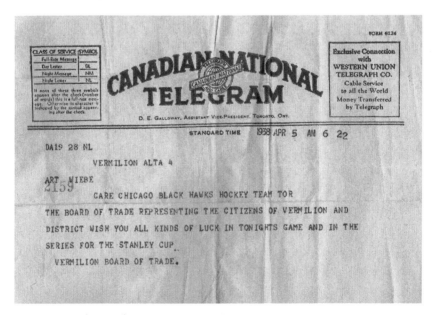

CANADIAN NATIONAL TELEGRAM

FORM 6124

CLASS OF SERVICE	SYMBOL
Full-Rate Message	
Day Letter	DL
Night Message	NM
Night Letter	NL

If none of these three symbols appears after the check (number of words) this is a full-rate message. Otherwise its character is indicated by the symbol appearing after the check.

D. E. GALLOWAY, Assistant Vice-President, Toronto, Ont.

Exclusive Connection with WESTERN UNION TELEGRAPH CO. Cable Service to all the World Money Transferred by Telegraph

STANDARD TIME   1938 APR 5 AM 6 22

DA19 28 NL

VERMILION ALTA 4

ART WIEBE

CARE CHICAGO BLACK HAWKS HOCKEY TEAM TOR

THE BOARD OF TRADE REPRESENTING THE CITIZENS OF VERMILION AND

DISTRICT WISH YOU ALL KINDS OF LUCK IN TONIGHTS GAME AND IN THE

SERIES FOR THE STANLEY CUP.

VERMILION BOARD OF TRADE.

The Vermilion (Alberta) Board of Trade also wished Art Wiebe well before the finals began. (Photo courtesy of the Art Wiebe family)

size rough checking in the defensive zone. His goal was to hinder the Maple Leafs' ability to set up plays. "He figured that the potent Toronto attack could be contained if the Maple Leaf centers were bottled up," wrote *Sports Illustrated*'s Herm Weiskopf on March 28, 1960.

The Blackhawks took to the ice before 13,737 Toronto fans. With tensions running extremely high, the first half of the opening period was especially physical. The Maple Leafs immediately began applying pressure on Moore, seeking to capitalize on the Blackhawks' minor-league netminder. Although Toronto's Drillon scored a rebound goal at 1:53 of the first period, Conn Smythe quickly realized that Alfie could hold his own against Toronto's sharpshooters.

Late in the period, Toronto's Turk Broda blocked a shot from Cully Dahlstrom, but Johnny Gottselig scored on the rebound, tying the game at 17:15. Although they had evened the score, the Blackhawks suffered a casualty during the first period when Mush March left the game with a pulled groin muscle. Still hot over the Kerr incident, more fireworks erupted after the first period when Bill Stewart exchanged choice words with bystander Hal Cotton.

In his April 7, 1938, article, Strickler said that Stewart mentioned "the Toronto racketeers who were Smythe's bodyguards." Like fire on gasoline, Stewart's words infuriated Cotton, who "rushed at the Hawk manager and let fly a punch that bruised Stewart's cheek. They exchanged several more blows before this bout was broken up, with Stewart still vowing that he wasn't through fighting and that the whole league would hear of the 'raw deal' his team had received."

Chicago's adrenaline rush continued when Paul Thompson received a pass from Earl Seibert and released a hard, 30-foot shot that slipped through Broda's legs, giving the Blackhawks a 2-1 lead at 1:50 of the second period. In the third period, the Maple Leafs tried to rush the Blackhawks' net during a Chicago line change. However, the momentum changed when Alex Levinsky poke-checked the puck away from Toronto's Bill Thoms. At the blue line, Gottselig recovered the puck and made a solo rush down the ice. The Chicago veteran scored his second goal of the game at 12:07, giving the Blackhawks a 3-1 victory.

Stewart's strategy appeared to be working for the Blackhawks. "They are a peculiar pack, but they really are working hard for their

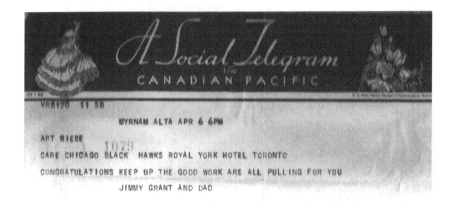

Art Wiebe's family sent him a congratulatory telegram as the Blackhawks fought their way through the Stanley Cup finals. (Photo courtesy of the Art Wiebe family)

scrappy manager and their stop-and-go style bothers the hurrying Leafs," wrote Munns. "Our young fellows can match speed with speed, but they are somewhat baffled by the Hawks' change of pace."

Alfie Moore had done such an exceptional job that the Blackhawks intended to use him again during the second game of the series. However, it was not to be. In "a second last-minute maneuver, with President Frank Calder of the National Hockey League as the pawn, Moore was declared ineligible for the second game," wrote Horton Trautman in the *Chicago Daily News*. "Paul Goodman, a young and earnest, but innocent and frightened lad who had never even seen a major-league hockey game, much less played in one, was ordered to be the Hawks' goalie."

Following his sole postseason appearance with the Blackhawks, Moore saw only limited NHL action. He played two games with the New York Americans in 1938–39 and one with the Detroit Red Wings in 1939–40. Later, Moore coached the Ontario Hockey League's (OHL) Galt Black Hawks in 1949–50.

As the Blackhawks prepared for game two, played in Toronto on April 7, Smythe and Stewart downplayed the blows they had exchanged. "As far as I'm concerned, the fights are all forgotten," Smythe said in the April 7, 1938, *Boston Globe*. Stewart provided a similar statement, explaining: "It was just one of those things that crop up in the heat of a moment."

"No hard feelings." Conn Smythe (left) and Bill Stewart (right) shake hands in Toronto on April 7, 1938. (City of Toronto Archives)

With Karakas still injured, substitute goalie Paul Goodman arrived by plane from Winnipeg. Goodman's regular experience as an NHL goaltender was limited to the Blackhawks. He suited up 52 times for the team, including 31 games in 1939–40 and 21 the following season. Born to Icelandic parents on February 25, 1905, in Selkirk, Manitoba, Goodman was an electrical contractor by trade. He became a partner in the Sargent Electric and Radio Co. Ltd. in 1927 and remained with the organization until his death from a heart attack on October 1, 1959, at age 54. Goodman also was a Winnipeg alderman who played an instrumental role in forming the city's bantam hockey league. He was inducted into the Manitoba Hockey Hall of Fame posthumously in 1985.

The Blackhawks found a replacement for injured Mush March in Pete Palangio, who arrived from North Bay, Ontario, and was still in good shape after helping the St. Louis Flyers win the AHA championship. The Maple Leafs stayed sharp with a brief drill 70 miles away, at the Preston Springs Resort. March and Karakas both returned home to Chicago for treatment of their respective injuries.

Mike Karakas and Paul Goodman pose for a publicity shot in front of the net. The "Professional Goalie" inscription on their sticks eliminates any possible confusion regarding their chosen occupation. (Photo courtesy of Ty Dilello/Manitoba Hockey Hall of Fame)

The second game was brutal and disheartening for Chicago. Under the impression that Alfie Moore would be in goal, Goodman was found in a movie theater as game time approached. This was likely sometime in the afternoon and not minutes before the action began, as some sources suggest.

The Maple Leafs got on the scoreboard first with a goal from Drillon at 1:42, but Earl Seibert tied the game with a Chicago goal at 8:46. Although Goodman allowed a long shot from Toronto's Harvey Jackson to slip through his legs during the seventh minute of the second period, the Blackhawks maintained a fighting chance until the middle of the third period when Drillon scored at 9:40. Toronto's George Parsons followed with two additional goals at 10:29 and 11:09.

In the *Chicago Daily News*, Horton Trautman wrote: "It was in this second game of the finals for the Stanley Cup that Red Horner, hockey's

A
SOCIAL
Message

CA293 68

BN CHICAGO ILL 7 1256P

PAUL GOODMAN

1017   CR W J TOBIN CHICAGO NATL HOCKEY TEAM ROYAL YORK HOTEL TOR.

DONT WORRY ABOUT TONIGHTS GAME JUST GET IN AND DO THE BEST

YOU CAN WE ARE ALL PULLING FOR YOU WIN LOSE OR DRAW ITS

ASKING AN AWFUL LOT OF YOU AND UNDER NO CIRCUMSTANCES WILL

YOU BE BLAMED FOR ANYTHING THAT HAPPENS ALSO REMEMBER THAT

ITS YOUR GREAT CHANCE TO SHOW THE STUFF THAT MADE YOU THE

OUTSTANDING GOALIE OF THE AMERICAN LEAGUE GOOD LUCK TO YOU.

FREDERIC MCLAUGHLIN.

This telegram from Frederic McLaughlin offered encouragement to Paul Goodman prior to game two of the Stanley Cup finals. (Photo courtesy of Ty Dilello/Manitoba Hockey Hall of Fame)

---

worst bad man for six years in succession, rammed Doc Romnes with the butt end of a stick, breaking the nose of the winner of the Lady Byng trophy for sportsmanship and clean play, and cut Roger Jenkins and Louie Trudel to the skull. The Horner attacks disorganized the Hawks and the Leafs won, 5 to 1."

Horner's handiwork increased the number of injured players on the Blackhawks' roster to 10. In addition to Karakas, March, Romnes, Jenkins, and Trudel, Johnny Gottselig, Cully Dahlstrom, Alex Levinsky, Art Wiebe, and Carl Voss also had sustained injuries. Wiebe was injured while sitting on the bench, the victim of a flying puck. "Battered and bandaged, the Chicago Blackhawks assembled what remained of their Stanley Cup contenders today and it was the sorriest looking hockey team ever to battle for the tarnished old mug," Steve Snider wrote for the United Press on April 9, 1938.

Back in the Windy City, injured Blackhawks reported to Garfield Park Community Hospital for evaluations, X-rays, stitches, and dia-

Paul Goodman (Photo courtesy of Ty Dilello/Manitoba Hockey Hall of Fame)

thermic treatments. Doctors outfitted the most seriously injured players with special equipment in preparation for game three. A reinforced
shoe, featuring a steel splint, was made for Karakas, while Doc Romnes
was given a mask to protect his nose, which was broken in three places.

Bill Stewart recalled the scene in Herm Weiskopf's March 28, 1960,
Sports Illustrated article: "The next day I went to the Garfield Park Hospital in Chicago to see my injured boys," he said. "It was like a scene from

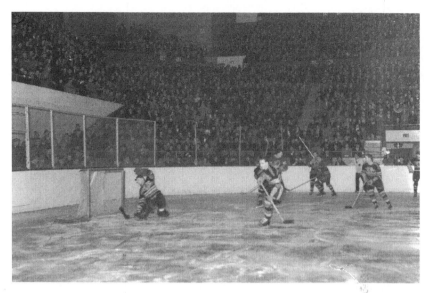

Paul Goodman defends Chicago's goal in game two of the Stanley Cup finals on April 7, 1938. (City of Toronto Archives)

a war movie. Half a dozen of them were laid out with cuts and bruises, and Doc Romnes, one of my centers, had a broken nose. I knew the boys were upset, so before the game I told them, 'Now listen, no matter what happened in Toronto, let's go out there to win this game, and don't look at it as a chance for revenge.'"

As they prepared for game three, the Blackhawks were likely glad to be back home. Beginning with a March 13 contest with Detroit, the team had played all but two of their last 11 games on the road. To that point, skating had been reserved for competition; on April 9, the team had its first practice session in 25 days. In addition to the players' wives, Alfie Moore, who had traveled to Chicago with the team, also was on hand to watch the practice. Before game three, which he attended as a guest of the Blackhawks, Moore was introduced to a cheering Chicago crowd and received a gold watch from Karakas, which players and other admirers had purchased for him as a gift.

"Doc's Revenge" is a fitting name for the series' third game at Chicago Stadium. *Chicago Tribune* sportswriter Edward Burns claimed that after Horner broke Romnes's nose in three places, Doc promised to retaliate in game three. "Romnes, it is recalled, served notice on the burly

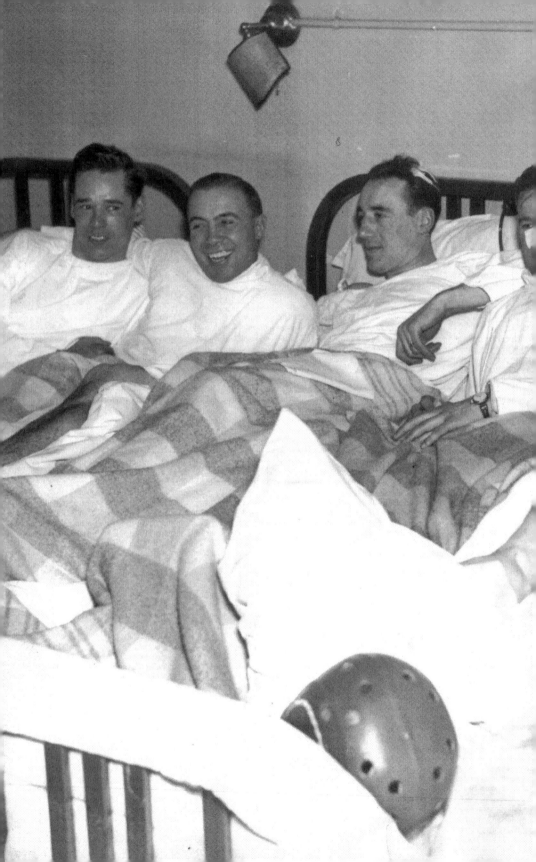

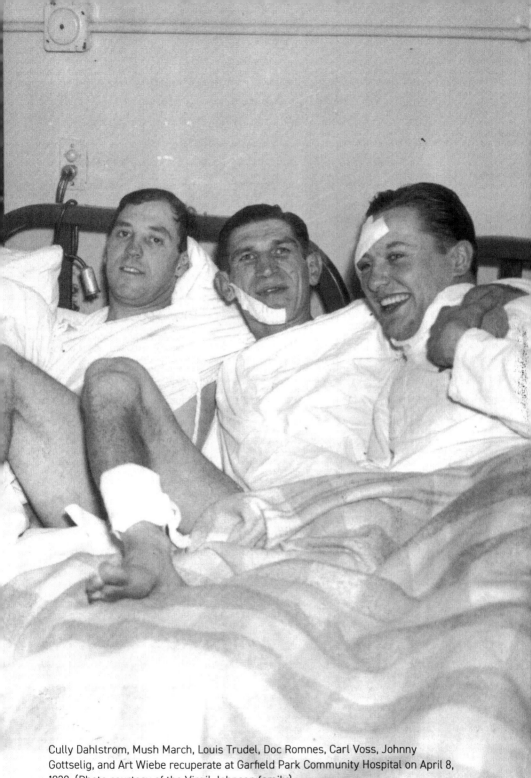

Cully Dahlstrom, Mush March, Louis Trudel, Doc Romnes, Carl Voss, Johnny Gottselig, and Art Wiebe recuperate at Garfield Park Community Hospital on April 8, 1938. (Photo courtesy of the Virgil Johnson family)

Leaf captain that he would 'cut off his head' the instant the game in Chicago, third of the final series, began," he wrote on December 9, 1938.

The contest was witnessed by 18,496 fans, who undoubtedly were attracted by the fairytale-like aura surrounding the team. Both the *Chicago Daily News* and *Chicago Daily Tribune* described this as the largest crowd to ever witness a professional hockey game. The larger crowd was possible because of extra seats that were placed in front of the boxes surrounding the rink. Game three was officiated by former Chicago Blackhawk Cecil "Babe" Dye and future NHL President Clarence Campbell.

With Karakas back in goal and Romnes wearing a Purdue University football helmet to protect his nose, the Blackhawks focused on evening the score with their nemesis. "Horner is a free style defense man, well-versed in every phase of hockey except the rules," wrote George Strickler in the April 10, 1938, *Chicago Daily Tribune*. "He is the Hawks' unanimous choice as Toronto's most valuable player. His outstanding series accomplishment to date, they are agreed, was the splintering of Romnes's nose. It was a work of art."

Instead of trying to win the opening faceoff when Campbell dropped the puck, Romnes went straight at Horner. Raising his stick in the air, he took a swing at the Toronto defenseman, who doubled over even though he had not been hit. Horner was helped off the ice by his teammates and trainer Tim Daly, who raced to his aid with smelling salts. In an April 12, 1938, article, sportswriter Horton Trautman said: "Red fell forward like a collapsed puppet and kept his head cushioned in his mittens until helped off the ice by his pals and Romnes was given a minor penalty for slashing." After the incident, Horner's rough edge was gone for the rest of the series.

"As I understand it, he never really touched Horner, but took a big swing and Horner just went down," recalls Romnes's daughter, Virginia Hansen. "All I can say is, my dad must have been pushed to the limit to do that, because he was always very mild-mannered, and he wasn't a big man. He was quite small, and that's why he had to be really fast and crafty with his stick and with the skating. I remember him talking about it [the Red Horner incident] and, after the fact, kind of chuckling because of the way it turned out."

Ironically, Romnes was traded to the Maple Leafs in 1938–39. "If you can imagine, Red Horner and the manager met him at the train, after that incident on the ice," says Hansen. "I remember my dad was quite surprised, but they shook hands and really became friends eventually, playing together. My dad proved himself, deserving of being up there [in Toronto] and earned his respect."

Romnes's penalty was followed by a second Chicago infraction when Mush March tripped Toronto's Bob Davidson. Looking back on the penalty years later, March described it as one of the toughest moments of his career. He joined Romnes in the penalty box, giving the Maple Leafs a two-man advantage. Capitalizing on the opportunity, Syl Apps gave Toronto an early lead, scoring on Karakas at 1:35.

In all, the first period of play was filled with nine penalties, including a major received by Toronto's George Parsons for dropping the gloves with Roger Jenkins. The atmosphere was electrified by a rowdy crowd, still angry over Horner's actions during game two. Prior to the game, Stadium employees had confiscated alcohol, along with rotten vegetables and other would-be projectiles, from patrons. Nevertheless, fighting spilled over into the crowd. Several fans were ejected, and Horner was a prime target of debris that had been smuggled into the arena.

After receiving a pass from Roger Jenkins, Carl Voss tied the game with a second period Chicago goal at 16:02. During the third period, Horner checked Jenkins and found himself in a near entanglement with the Chicago defenseman. Horner's reluctance to drop the gloves prompted chants of "Horner's yellow" from the crowd. At one point, Blackhawks' stick boy Dan Cunningham was ejected for taking a swing at Horner.

Romnes ultimately fired a long, hard shot past Broda at 15:55 of the third period, securing victory for the Blackhawks. After going in, the puck bounced back out of the cage and onto the ice. When the goal judge's red light signified a goal, an enraged Horner attempted to assault goal judge John McLean. He was restrained by Chicago players while ushers encircled McLean and protected him for the rest of the game.

The Blackhawks emerged physically unscathed from the rough-and-tumble third contest. With only one match standing between them and the world championship, the underdogs prepared to face off against Toronto for a fourth time. In the calm before the storm, the team took some time to relax before the next game. Defenseman Earl Seibert bought ice cream sodas for two young fans at the Guyon Hotel. Art Wiebe and Louis Trudel read through newspaper articles about their accomplishments thus far.

In the April 12, 1938, *Chicago Daily News*, Bill Stewart revealed how he instilled a winning spirit in what the paper now called the "miracle team":

"Although a lot of people hate to admit it, I had every right to know a lot about hockey when I took over the Hawks," he said. "I officiated in hockey games for many years and I had a lot of opportunities to observe different systems of play and their chances for success. Experience as an athlete and as a coach in football, baseball, track and college hockey gave me a great fund of knowledge of athletes, gave me a working basis on how to handle them.

"The Hawks team that I took over was made up of a number of great veterans and a number of possible youngsters," he continued. "I spent a good deal of the season getting the men—particularly the veterans—to have faith in my ideas. Now they're seeing them work out right. I had to go through quite a fight on the matter of conditioning the men. Some people think that physical condition is everything in that constant practice and 'P.T.'—that's physical training—is the fundamental secret.

"I'm not against 'P.T.,' but I never did believe that older athletes should burn up their energies by dull exercises," Stewart added. "Older athletes have their skills; they know how to keep in condition and games are enough actual exercise for them. By having them rest between games—and hockey games are played often enough to give any man enough exercise—all my men have full funds of energy.

"What is more, they're eager to play when each game starts," concluded Stewart. "I really think my Hawks are still getting fun out of the game— even after all the trying months of the season and the strain of play-off games. I know the players of most of the other teams were sick and tired of the game by the end of the season. They were just doing dull jobs of work, not

Bill Stewart is surrounded by his band of scrappy, determined Blackhawks. (Photo courtesy of the Virgil Johnson family)

playing a game. That system of conserving the men's energy between games, instead of expending it, plus certain plans of actual play—marked mainly by consistently pushing the puck forward and keeping between it and our goal— is what makes the Hawks the team they are today—wise, scrappy, skillful and full of competitive and winning spirit."

Even Horner acknowledged how formidable the Blackhawks were as competitors, commenting: "The real surprise, though, is that the Hawks did so poorly earlier in the season. The Blackhawks are a darn good hockey team now. Plenty of good players are on the team and it doesn't seem possible that they should have been so far down in the league standing during the season."

Stewart also responded to criticisms that the Blackhawks played an unnecessarily rough game against Toronto. "The Hawks play the cleanest game in the league as proved by the figures on time spent in the penalty box," he said. "They are famous among other players for avoiding roughness. The fact that they tore into the Leafs Sunday night only proves that they were acting in self-defense. Toronto had cut them to pieces the previous Thursday, and the Hawks were out to put a stop to such tactics. They did."

During the regular season, Horner had amassed 82 penalty minutes (second in the NHL), while Blackhawks' penalty minute leader Earl Seibert had 38. As a team, Toronto had 404 penalty minutes to Chicago's 240. "They will play any way the Leafs want tonight—straight hockey or blow for blow," said Stewart. "It's up to the Leafs. Let them choose. I have discouraged retaliation all season, but my men must be allowed to protect themselves. Red Horner, the Leaf captain, cut four of our men in Toronto, and the only way to defend yourself against him after that is to take the fight to him. This has been done. It will not be done again if he shows he has learned his lesson."

The sun rose over Chicago shortly after 5 a.m. on Tuesday, April 12. It was a primary election day in the city and throughout Illinois. The weather was fair, cool, and partly cloudy. The morning of game four, Chicago citizens opened the sports page of the *Chicago Daily Tribune* to read George Strickler's column, which began: "Tradition wobbles on putty legs today, a set-up for a finishing jolt by young men engaged in proving they do come back. Up from the depths of the National league, hand over hand along a trail of adversity, the Hawks sit poised on the threshold to the throne room of hockey."

After arriving at Chicago Stadium, coach Stewart learned that a last-minute change in minor officials had been made. When Conn Smythe expressed concerns about the performance of John McLean and Fritz Pike in game three, NHL President Frank Calder ordered a new goal judge and penalty timer be sent to Chicago from New York. The Blackhawks were unaware of the new officials' names at game time.

"Smythe reported to Calder in Montreal that the puck had not gone into the net on Doc Romnes's shot which won Sunday night's game, 2 to 1, for the Hawks," wrote Charles Bartlett in the April 13, 1938, *Chicago Daily Tribune*. "Pike was accused of sending Red Horner on the ice before the big defense man's time had expired. The premature return resulted in another penalty for Horner."

An energized crowd of 17,205 fans filled Chicago Stadium to wit-

Cully Dahlstrom scored a key goal in Chicago's 1938 Stanley Cup victory over Toronto. (Photo courtesy of the Cully Dahlstrom family)

ness game four—one of the most unforgettable contests in professional sports history. Among them were Frederic McLaughlin's daughter, Barbara, who had returned home from college on the East Coast to see the action.

Three fights erupted during the first period, which was characterized by the rough play seen throughout the series. About five minutes into the game, the line of Cully Dahlstrom, Jack Shill, and Louie Trudel went on the attack. After Dahlstrom got the puck past Toronto's defense, Trudel and Shill both attempted to score. Their shots were blocked by Turk Broda, but Dahlstrom put Chicago on the scoreboard first with a goal at 5:52. Drillon answered for Toronto with a goal at 8:26.

Chicago's Carl Voss broke the tie with a late second period goal at 16:45, assisted by Gottselig and Jenkins. About a minute later, Shill

pulled the Blackhawks ahead with a remarkable, unassisted goal at 17:58. The Chicago defenseman fired what then was the longest goal ever scored at Chicago Stadium when he lifted the puck into the air far from the Toronto cage, with estimates ranging from 110 to 150 feet.

A March 28, 1960, Sports Illustrated article explained that, as a defensive measure, Stewart had decided to use up time during the remainder of the second period by having Shill fire the puck from near center ice. "Shill didn't wait to get to center ice though," wrote Herm Weiskopf. "He lofted the puck high into the air while still some 150 feet from the Toronto net. Broda came out of the cage, confidently dropped to his knees for what appeared to be an easy stop, and then stared in disbelief as the puck skipped over his stick and into the net." With a 3-1 lead, Chicago began playing conservatively and no penalties were called during the second period.

As the Blackhawks fought to keep their lead, excitement continued to build throughout the Stadium. "The crowd was in hysterics throughout the struggle, springing up and down as often as an overweight businessman taking exercises to reduce [his weight]," penned sportswriter Bob Stanton. Describing the noisy fans, Stanton said: "Cowbells, sleigh bells, horns, oranges, lemons, torn papers and confetti were part of their equipment in addition to their vocal cords. At times the rink looked like a street after a carnival, and several times the fans appeared willing to climb out of their seats and join the fighting players."

The crowd's "equipment" not only was reserved for moments of excitement, but also pent-up anger toward Horner. Cards and paper were flung into the air as the crowd chanted, "We Want Horner!" At one point, the shower of debris delayed the game while the ice was cleared off.

With electricity in the air, the game progressed to the third and final period. On the Chicago bench, Bill Stewart and the players began counting the remaining time on the clock. At 10:40 p.m., Mush March shouted to his teammates that only five minutes remained. With victory in reach, Stewart motioned March onto the ice, and shortly thereafter the forward scored a pressure-relieving fourth goal for Chicago at 16:24.

_____

(opposite) Toronto Maple Leafs goaltender Turk Broda. (Photo courtesy of the Boston Public Library, Leslie Jones Collection)

At this point, Stewart instructed Johnny Gottselig to run out the rest of the game by playing keep-away with the Maple Leafs. "And that's just what he did," Stewart recalled in Weiskopf's *Sports Illustrated* article. "He skated around those Toronto players as if they weren't there. I never saw anything like it."

The Blackhawks had accomplished what few thought possible, humiliating the Maple Leafs. Following the stunning victory, the Stadium crowd went wild with excitement. The Blackhawks gathered at center ice, surrounded by photographers. Although they were champions, the Stanley Cup remained physically out of reach; the silver chalice was nowhere to be found. Initially, some believed that NHL President Frank Calder had ordered the Stanley Cup sent to Toronto, assuming the Maple Leafs would be the ultimate victors.

Cully Dahlstrom's daughter, Jean McKean, remembers her father talking about the trophy's absence. "The Cup wasn't there," she says. "They didn't think they had a chance; they were a Cinderella team. They were all shocked that it was not there when they won. It was terrible. The crowd stayed for hours, evidently, celebrating. No one left the Stadium; it was so, so exciting!"

In an article that appeared the day after the game, sportswriter Dee Sparr wrote: "Sending the trophy to the losers was only in keeping with the manner in which the whole of the series has been conducted. From start to finish, it bordered on the farcical and was probably the most mismanaged sports event ever conducted. Rules were broken with ease. Officials were replaced at the mere suggestion of the heads of the Toronto club."

Most of the Maple Leafs showed good sportsmanship following the Chicago victory, exchanging congratulations at center ice. Toronto's Harvey "Busher" Jackson saluted the Stadium crowd and threw his stick up to the mezzanine level, where one fan recovered a valuable souvenir. Alex Levinsky skated up to Red Horner, his hand extended in friendship. Although Horner shook it, that was the extent of his congratulations to the Blackhawks. "The big Leaf defense man, who played without his proverbial skill or spirit in this last game, limped off toward the dressing room at the end, too dejected to join his teammates in congratulations to the new champions," wrote Stanton.

Left to Right: Alex Levinsky, coach Bill Stewart, Mush March, and Lou Trudel
celebrate winning the Stanley Cup at Chicago Stadium on April 12, 1938. (Le Studio
du Hockey/Hockey Hall of Fame)

With goalie Mike Karakas on the shoulders of his teammates,
and Stewart being carried by Mush March and Alex Levinsky, the players skated off the ice, receiving congratulations from owner Frederic
McLaughlin on their way to the dressing room, where the celebration
continued. Johnny Gottselig, trainer Packy Schwartz, and Pete Palangio
lifted Stewart onto their shoulders, posing before newspaper photographers for another victory photo.

Bill Stewart shared his observations regarding the team's victory in
an April 14, 1938, United Press article that ran in the *Berkshire Eagle*. "The
human element has ruined many a plot—but not ours," he said. "Everything broke just right—even to the nose on Doc Romnes's face. That
broken nose had almost as much to do with beating the Maple Leafs as
all our plans. It fired up the whole team."

In the same article, Stewart reflected on the strategy he had employed throughout the playoffs, and the end result, commenting: "We

A private celebration is held for players, their family members, and friends following the 1938 Stanley Cup victory. (Photo courtesy of the Mike Karakas family)

might have looked unorthodox, but there was plenty of reason for everything we did. Anyway, it proves Americans can play hockey. Eight of my boys—Romnes, Alex Levinsky, Cully Dahlstrom, Louis Trudel, Roger Jenkins, Carl Voss, Virgil Johnson and Mike Karakas—were born on this side of the border. M-m-m. And so was I."

Jenkins, who lost a bet similar to the one he made with goaltender Chuck Gardiner in 1934, wheeled Karakas down State Street in a wheelbarrow before thousands of onlookers. While recapping the Stanley Cup finals, Chicago's veteran players attributed a significant share of the team's success to younger players. In addition to Dahlstrom and Shill, on April 14, 1938, *Chicago Daily Tribune* columnist George Strickler emphasized that defenseman Art Wiebe's play "was one of the bright spots of the series, eclipsed only by that of Earl Seibert, who comes to notice more often for his offensive work."

After the historic victory, players were soon making their way back home. Jenkins's departure to Edmonton was delayed only by a search for his jersey, which had disappeared. Dahlstrom returned to his parents' home in Minneapolis and took some time to relax before taking a trip out West. After arriving back in Calgary, Paul Thompson attended the final game of the Allan Cup series. He was congratulated by admirers, who saw Western Canada's Trail Smoke Eaters defeat Eastern Canada's Cornwall Flyers and win the country's senior amateur hockey championship.

Karakas worked at a gas station in Eveleth during the summer. The December 10, 1938, issue of *Collier's* joked that patrons "tabbed him as a lazy clockwatcher, because he would pause at regular intervals to sneak a peek at a gold watch. He was merely trying to make himself believe it all by rereading the inscription on the back: Black Hawks—World Champions 37–38 MIKE KARAKAS."

As Karakas glanced reassuringly at the gold watch, his image on boxes of Wheaties cereal confirmed Iron Mike's champion status, long before such endorsements were commonplace, or lucrative. "Today, if you get your picture on the Wheaties box you're a millionaire automatically," says Mike's daughter, Joan Karakas. "I asked my mother what my father got, and she said, 'Lots of cartons of Wheaties.'"

As a Stanley Cup champion, Dahlstrom received a $2,250 bonus and, like his teammates, a gold medal and an engraved watch. Years after the victory, he offered his thoughts on what enabled the team to keep winning in the playoffs, despite such a poor regular season. "It was determination by the individual players," he said. "We seemed to have a group together there that didn't want to lose. And as such we played hard, and probably above our natural ability. That's why we won. When we went up to Toronto, they were kings of the hockey world at that time. We lost the first game quite badly, but then we got together and took control, so to speak, and we beat 'em. It's determination, and the guys that don't want to get beat, they usually win!"

Dahlstrom's daughter, Jean McKean, explains that her father's winning spirit has echoed through generations of his family: "He would always say to his three girls, any time that we had anything going on that we were worried about, or if we're going to make the team, or whatever, he would say: 'You're a Dahlstrom; you can do it!' We always say that to each other. I say to our kids, 'You're a Dahlstrom; you can do it!' That's kind of how he felt. What he was going after, he'd do. He excelled at

Photos of defenseman Art Wiebe's 1938 Stanley Cup medal. (Photos courtesy of the Art Wiebe family)

whatever he chose to do, whether it was school, or when he came out West and became a realtor and a broker and opened up his own office."

On April 14, Bill Stewart, Doc Romnes, and Jack Shill were present at the team's office when a crate arrived from Detroit. Inside, the men found the object that was emblematic of their accomplishment: the Stanley Cup. Apparently, the Red Wings, who were the previous season's champions, had held onto the trophy for shipment to Toronto, operating on the assumption that Chicago could not possibly win. The following season, Chicago Stadium welcomed its largest opening night crowd to date on November 3, 1938. Throngs of excited fans saw Chicago Cubs manager Gabby Hartnett publicly present the Stanley Cup to Stewart as a world championship pennant was unfurled over center ice.

Life slowly returned to normal in Chicago. The *Garfieldian*, a newspaper circulated throughout the area where many of the players lived, announced that a massive Easter egg hunt and egg-rolling contest was scheduled in Garfield Park on Saturday, April 16. Some of the remaining players and their families may have been among the roughly 5,000 attendees. That Sunday, Frederic McLaughlin's wife, Irene Castle, hosted a luncheon for actors Burgess Meredith and Lillian Gish, who were performing in the Broadway production *The Star-Wagon* in Chicago.

On April 20, Major McLaughlin announced that team captain Paul Thompson (the NHL's American Division scoring leader in 1937–38) would be assistant manager and assistant coach in 1938–39. Thompson,

Coach Bill Stewart embraces the Stanley Cup, on display at the Graemere Hotel on August 15, 1938. (Le Studio du Hockey/Hockey Hall of Fame)

Boston Bees 1st baseman Elbie Fletcher with National League umpire Bill Stewart in front of the dugout at Bees Field in 1937. (Photo courtesy of the Boston Public Library, Leslie Jones Collection)

then 30, would continue to play as well, receiving the NHL's maximum salary of $7,500. By this time, McLaughlin had signed contracts with several key players for the following season, including Mush March, Bill Mackenzie, Alex Levinsky, Roger Jenkins, and Johnny Gottselig.

Shortly after the Stanley Cup victory, Stewart resumed his work as a professional baseball umpire, returning to his hometown of Boston to umpire the city series between the Red Sox and the Bees. "It was the Depression, and he was not a college-educated guy," his grandson, Bill Stewart III, once recalled. After purchasing a new station wagon, Doc Romnes gave Stewart and his wife a ride to the train station, before heading home to White Bear Lake, Minnesota.

Stewart had become one of the year's most famous sports figures by leading the Blackhawks to Stanley Cup glory in his first season as an NHL coach. Even more remarkable, he was the first American-born manager to accomplish this feat. When Stewart's train arrived late at

The 1937–38 Stanley Cup Champion Chicago Blackhawks. (Hockey Hall of Fame)

Boston's South Station on April 15, the coach was mobbed by approximately 200 supporters. From there, in the company of his 18-year-old son, Bill, Jr., and 80-year-old mother, Margaret, Stewart and his wife traveled to the state house under police escort to meet Massachusetts Lieutenant Governor Francis E. Kelly.

Although Stewart's contract ran for another season, he was behind the Chicago bench for only 21 games in 1938–39. The Blackhawks won just 12 games that season (12-28-8), missing the playoffs. Following Stewart's departure, Paul Thompson was named head coach.

A January 3, 1939, *Chicago Daily News* article by John Carmichael explained that Stewart was dismissed during a lengthy meeting that included Thompson, Bill Tobin, and Frederic McLaughlin. "Such a change was reported to have been almost completed more than a month ago when, after the Hawks were defeated 2 to 0 in Boston on Dec. 6, the managerial job is said to have been offered to Thompson," he wrote. "At that time Thompson, it is said, was reluctant to have Stewart ousted so abruptly after his feat of managing the Hawks to an 'impossible' victory in the Stanley Cup series a year ago."

Paul Stewart once explained that an incident involving McLaughlin and his grandfather contributed to the coach's demise. "The Major had come down [to the locker room] and was berating a player in between periods," he explained. "My grandfather pitched him, and he fired him for that. They had a slow start, I guess, but there was also perhaps a little undermining. I was told by several people that the guy that came in after him, Paul Thompson, was sort of working behind him a little bit. That may have been so, and it may not."

Beyond their locker room clash, other factors contributed to the breakdown in McLaughlin and Stewart's working relationship. "The Major wanted him to coach from the press box at one point, and he was fired, as he was quoted in the paper in 1939, because he wouldn't take orders," Stewart's other grandson, Bill Stewart III, once said. "My father told me the story that when he walked into the office, the Major said: 'William, how are you?' 'Good, Major.' 'You're fired.' And that was it. He couldn't use the word 'fired' because Mrs. Stewart didn't like it, so he chose 'released.' In the long run, my grandfather was pretty smart when he signed his contract, because he signed for two years; he got two years out of the deal, $6,500 a year."

During the mid-1990s, Paul Stewart credited his grandfather for having revolutionary ideas, explaining: "He used forwards on the power play. They did a lot of crisscrossing. They played the type of game they're playing now."

"He had an idea about the game," said Bill Stewart III. "It's just that he was an American in a totally Canadian game. At the time it held him back because I don't think anybody took him seriously. They kind of did after [he won the Cup], but I've read books by various and sundry people that kind of belittle him because of the Major's reputation, being eccentric, and because of my grandfather's reputation of being a tough battler and the flukiness of it, the Alfie Moore part of it. They've kind of belittled that team, and also that they had the worst record. . . . The Hawks went in with a bad record but they won the Cup and nobody can ever take that away from them."

As the thirties concluded and the 1940s began, the Blackhawks would slowly lose their punch, despite possessing some of the best talent in the league. During the late 1950s, a new generation of super-

In October 1938, the Blackhawks gathered in Chicago before heading to training camp in Champaign, Illinois. Before departing, some players spent time with the Stanley Cup won by the previous season's team. Front (left to right): Ab DeMarco, Paul Goodman, and Phil Besler. Rear: Johnny Gottselig, coach Paul Thompson, and Alex Levinsky. (Photo courtesy of Ty Dilello/Manitoba Hockey Hall of Fame)

stars like Bobby Hull, Stan Mikita, and Glenn Hall emerged in Chicago. These players would bring a third Stanley Cup to the Windy City nearly a quarter-century later, in 1961. However, the Blackhawks' victories in the 1930s, especially the highly improbable, awe-inspiring story of 1938, will forever stand as crowning achievements in Chicago sports history.

In the fall of 1938, the Blackhawks carry the Stanley Cup won by the previous season's team in front of Chicago's Bowman Dairy Company. Several members of the 1937–38 team are pictured, including Paul Goodman, Johnny Gottselig, Carl Voss, Cully Dahlstrom, Alex Levinsky (holding Cup), Roger Jenkins, Jack Shill, Bill MacKenzie, Art Wiebe, and Paul Thompson. (Photo courtesy of the Virgil Johnson family)

Left to Right: Earl Seibert, Marty Burke, Tom Drift, Alex Levinsky, and Art Wiebe pose for a photo in Nett Lake, Minnesota, in 1938. That fall, the team held its training camp in nearby Hibbing, Minnesota. (Photo courtesy of the Art Wiebe family)

Bibliography

30 Memorable Games Played by Chicago's Black Hawks. Cary, IL: Dynamic Promotions, 1962.

2011–2012 Chicago Blackhawks Media Guide. Chicago: Chicago Blackhawks, 2011.

Barry, Howard. "Maj. M'Laughlin Explains Hawks' 1934 Success." *Chicago Tribune*, February 3, 1934, 20.

Bartlett, Charles. "Hawks Whip Detroit, 2 to 1, in 2D Overtime." *Chicago Daily Tribune*, April 4, 1934, 25.

———. "Hawks Whip Toronto, 3-2; Clinch 2D Place." *Chicago Tribune*, March 19, 1934, 19.

———. "Hawks Win 2D Cup Game; Beat Wings, 4 to 1." *Chicago Daily Tribune*, April 6, 1934, 31.

———. "Mush March Drops Hockey Stick for Linesman's Job." *Chicago Tribune*, February 19, 1953, 72.

———. "Surprise! (For Whom?) Hawks Pick Gottselig." *Chicago Tribune*, April 26, 1945, 25.

Beales, Richard. "Earl Seibert: Hockey's Forgotten Superstar." *Hockey News*, February 17, 1995, 11.

Benjamin, Susan S. "The Midwest Athletic Club." National Register of Historic Places Inventory—Nomination Form, October 5, 1983.

"Bill MacKenzie." Hockey Hall of Fame: Toronto, ON. https://www.hhof.com/LegendsOfHockey/jsp/LegendsMember.jsp?mem=P196303&type=Player&page=bio&list=ByName.

"Blackhawks Hold Hard Scrimmage to Test Defense." *Chicago Daily Tribune*, October 19, 1937, 20.

Borenstein, Seth. "Donald P. McFadyen, 83, Judge, Played Five Years in NHL." *Sun-Sentinel* (FL), May 29, 1990, 6B.

Burke, Tim. "Conn Smythe Was Heart, Soul of Leafs." *Gazette* (Montreal, QC), November 20, 1980, 13.

Burns, Edward. "Blackhawks Battle Bruins to Tie, 0 to 0." *Chicago Tribune*, January 12, 1934, 2.

———. "Hawks Take Up That Detroit Matter Tonight." *Chicago Tribune*, November 30, 1933, 43.

———. "Hawks Trade Doc Romnes to Toronto for Bill Thoms." *Chicago Tribune*, December 9, 1938, 31.

———. "Russia's Contribution to Hawks Is Adept at Other Sports." *Chicago Sunday Tribune,* January 8, 1939, 27.

———. "Scout Farrell Takes Boss to Hawks' Camp." *Chicago Daily Tribune,* October 25, 1933, 25.

———. "Stewart Sees Improved Band of Blackhawks." *Chicago Daily Tribune,* October 20, 1937, 21.

Callahan, Marya. 2020. Telephone interview by author. Digital recording, January 15.

Carmichael, John P. "Crowd Stood and Cheered Gottselig." *Winnipeg Free Press* (Winnipeg, MB), March 23, 1946, 16.

———. "Title Unknown." *Chicago Daily News,* January 3, 1939.

Carveth, Jack. "March's Goal in Overtime Wins Stanley Cup for Chicago. Only Score Registered with Goodfellow in Box." *Detroit Free Press,* April 11, 1934, 17.

———. "Red Wings Confident They Will Even Series." *Detroit Free Press,* April 10, 1934, 17.

Castanier, Bill, and Gregory Parker. "Taffy Abel. A Sault Sensation." *Michigan History,* March/April 2013, 49-53.

Castle, Irene Enzinger. *Castles in the Air.* Garden City, NY: Doubleday & Company, 1958.

Chambers, Antonia. *Before the Echoes Fade: The Story of Charlie Gardiner.* McLean, VA: Lanark Press, 2006.

"Chicago Casts Votes Quietly; Only 7 Arrests." *Chicago Daily Tribune,* April 11, 1934, 5.

Chicago Stadium Review, January 1, 1939.

"Chuck Gardiner, Blackhawks' Goalie, Dies." *Chicago Daily Tribune,* June 14, 1934, 25.

Cohn, Marv. "Hawks Run Wild in Hockey Match." *Daily Illini,* November 4, 1933.

Coleman, Jim. "Coleman's Column." *Lethbridge Herald* (Lethbridge, AB), December 7, 1950.

———. "Old Sporting Friends Ivy, Apps, Relocated." *Ottawa Citizen* (Ottawa, ON), March 3, 1971, 22.

Conacher, Lionel. "Black Hawks Play According to Plans." *Windsor Star* (Windsor, ON), April 6, 1934, 5.

Cordry, George. "Dahlstrom Recalls His Stanley Cup Days." *Times Advocate,* May 19, 1982.

Coulter, Art. 1989. Transcript of telephone interview with Antonia Chambers, 2 January.

Dahlstrom, Cully. 1993. Telephone interview by author. Tape recording, 12 November.

Dahlstrom, Cully. "Competition at Early Age Key to Hockey Success— Dahlstrom." *Chicago Times,* date unknown.

Dahlstrom, Gladys. Family correspondence, November 22, 1938.

Dahlstrom, Gladys. Family correspondence, November 30, 1938.

"Dahlstrom Hero; Has Broken Jaw." *Detroit Free Press,* December 11, 1937.

Damata, Ted. "Hockey's Wildest Series—Slaughter on Ice." *Chicago Tribune Magazine,* March 25, 1962, 30-32.

De Geer, Vern. "Hockey's Miracle Man." *Gazette* (Montreal, QC), February 20, 1964, 26.

Devaney, John, and Burt Goldblatt. *The Stanley Cup: A History*. Chicago: Rand McNally, 1975.

Diamond, Dan. *Total Hockey. The Official Encyclopedia of the National Hockey League*. New York: Total Sports, 1998.

Dotson, Perry. "Two Great Competitors; Virg, Cully Stand Alone." N.p., n.d.

Drukenbrod, M. F. "Druke Says: Hockey Owners They're So Jolly and So Different." *Detroit Free Press*, January 26, 1934, 17.

"Earl Seibert." Hockey Hall of Fame: Toronto, ON. https://www.hhof.com/LegendsOfHockey/jsp/LegendsMember.jsp?mem=P196303&type=Player&page=bio&list=ByName.

"East Wins Final Hockey Exhibition." *Daily Illini*, November 5, 1933.

Falls, Joe. "Hockey Corner." *Hockey News*, December 24, 1982, 12.

Fitzsimmons, Jack. 1995. Telephone interview by author. Tape recording, 29 April.

Gallagher, Jim. "Hawks Try Ace Rookie Tonight." *Chicago American*, January 6, 1938.

———. "Stewart in Debut as Pilot." *Chicago American*, November 4, 1937.

Gaston, Tom. 1995. Interview by author. Tape recording. Toronto, ON, 29 November.

Goldstein, Richard. "Art Coulter, 91, Defenseman and Captain of 1940 Rangers." *New York Times*, October 20, 2000. https://www.nytimes.com/2000/10/20/sports/art-coulter-91-defenseman-and-captain-of-1940-rangers.html.

Goldstick, Tiger. "Biography of Art Wiebe" (unpublished), 1971.

Graham, Tommy. "Art Wiebe Rises from Country Boy to Grand Star in Major Hockey." *Edmonton Journal* (Edmonton, AB), January 1936.

Hansen, Virginia. 2017. Telephone interview by author. Tape recording, 25 July.

"Hawks Follow Rules in Drill; It's a Shock." *Chicago Daily Tribune*, October 16, 1937, 26.

"Hawks Upset Toronto in Wild Opener." *Boston Globe*, April 6, 1938, 19.

Hemstock, Mark. 2020. E-mail to author. 9 February.

"Hockey Jockey." *Collier's*, January 4, 1936, 22, 37.

"Hockey Star Found Drowned; Police Probe Murder Theory." *Edmonton Journal* (Edmonton, AB), August 7, 1934, 1.

Holst, Doc. "Four American-Born Stars Seeking Red Wing Positions. Adams and Norris Wondering Just What McLaughlin Would Give for Them." *Detroit Free Press*, October 14, 1937, 22.

"Jack Leswick, Hockey Star, Dies in River." *Winnipeg Tribune* (Winnipeg, MB), August 7, 1934, 3.

Jewett, Ruth, and Jeannie McKeane. 2015. Telephone interview by author. Tape recording, 26 October.

Johnson, Edwin MC K. "Art Wiebe, Hawk Torpedo, Bounces Rangers Tonight." Source unknown, March 9, 1939.

Johnson, Virgil. Correspondence with Mr. & Mrs. E. A. Johnson, year unknown, November 18.

Karakas, Joan. 2017. Telephone interview by author. Tape recording, 26 June.

Kessler, Gene. "Ice on the Side." *Liberty Magazine*, February 5, 1938, 21.

"Leading Sports Figures Pay Tribute to 'Big Train.'" *Ottawa Journal* (Ottawa, ON), May 27, 1954, 25.

Leah, Vince. 1989. Transcript of in-person interview with Antonia Chambers, 15 June.

Let's Take an Afternoon Off with the Blackhawks!" *Chicago Sunday Tribune*, February 2, 1936.

Lieberman, J. Benjamin. "Horner Declares Game Was 'Swell'; Thinks Illini Spirit of Former Years Returning." *Daily Illini*, October 15, 1933.

Liscombe, Carl. 1996. Telephone interview by author. Tape recording, 20 February.

Loranger, Phil. *If They Played Hockey in Heaven—The Jack Adams Story*. Marjoguyhen Publishing Company, 1976.

Mahoney, Greg. "Johnny Gottselig Remembers." *Hockey*, April 1979.

Mann, Arthur. "Official Business." *Collier's*, January 1, 1938, 25, 35.

———. "Yankee Invasion." *Collier's*, December 10, 1938, 11, 42-43.

"Many Pay Tribute to Conacher." *Lethbridge Herald* (Lethbridge, AB), May 27, 1954, 7.

March, Harold. 1996. Telephone interview by author. Tape recording, 1 February.

March, Harold. "Toughest Spot I Was Ever In." *Chicago Tribune*, February 9, 1958, 43.

McLaughlin, Frederic. "ON ICE ~ and HOT." *American Legion Monthly*, Vol. 20, No. 2, February 1936, 26-27, 44-47.

Milks, James. "Well, You Found Me. Congratulations!" Society for International Hockey Research, October 15, 2016. https://sihrhockey.org/__a/public/column.cfm?cid=2&aid=448.

Munns, Tommy. "Hawks Crowd Zero Hour, Dallying in Dressing-Room While Maple Leafs Warm Up." *Toronto Globe and Mail*, date unknown.

———. "Moore Replaces Hurt Karakas After Fight." *Toronto Globe and Mail*, date unknown.

Murdoch, Murray. 1989. Transcript of telephone interview with Antonia Chambers, 15 January.

"Odds on Leafs Are Shortened. No Better Than Even on Winning Series. Managers Forget Fights and Concentrate on Game." *Boston Globe*, April 7, 1938, 22.

Patton, Paul. "Where Are They Now? Don McFadyen." *Toronto Globe and Mail*, May 9, 1986.

"Playoffs for Hocky [sic] Title to Start Tonight." *Chicago Daily Tribune*, March 20, 1934, 23.

Quackenbush, Bill. 1996. Letter to author. 4 February.

"Red Wings Work on Chicago Ice." *Ottawa Citizen* (Ottawa, ON), April 7, 1934, 13.

Riley, Don. "Untitled." *St. Paul Pioneer Press*, March 7, 1985.

Robertson, John. 1995. Interview by author. Tape recording. Chicago, IL, 29 April.

Rockwell, Tod. "Wings Cast Off Pall of Defeat." *Detroit Free Press*, April 4, 1934, 17.

Rothenberg, Matt. "A Hockey Hero and the AAGPBL." Cooperstown, NY: National Baseball Hall of Fame and Museum. https://baseballhall.org/discover-more/stories/short-stops/johnny-gottselig-and-the-all-american-girls-professional-baseball-league.

———. "#Shortstops: Bill Stewart's Career as an Official Swept Through MLB, NHL." Cooperstown, NY: National Baseball Hall of Fame and Museum. https://baseballhall.org/discover/short-stops/mlb-and-nhl-official-bill-stewart.

Schultz, Randy. "Cully Dahlstrom: One of America's Hockey Pioneers." *Hockey News*, May 24, 1985.

Schwieterman, Joseph P. *Terminal Town.* Lake Forest, IL: Lake Forest College Press, 2014.

Snider, Steve. "10 Blackhawks Crippled." United Press, April 9, 1938.

———. "Chicago's Stanley Cup Victory Shows Americans Can Play Hockey." *Berkshire Eagle* (Pittsfield, Berkshire, MA), April 14, 1938, 20.

Sparr, Dee. "Dahlstrom, 3 Veterans Star in 4-1 Victory." Source and Date Unknown.

Stanton, Bob. "Hawks Beat Leafs at Own Game to Win Stanley Cup." Source Unknown, April 13, 1938.

Stewart, Bill. "Untitled." *Chicago Times*, April 1938.

Stewart, Bill III. 1995. Telephone interview by author. Tape recording, 27 February.

Stewart, Paul. 1995. Telephone interview by author. Tape recording.

Stewart, Paul. 1996. Telephone interview by author. Tape recording, March 4.

Strickler, George. "Blackhawks Have Hockey Title, but Stanley Cup's in Toronto." *Chicago Daily Tribune*, April 14, 1938, 23.

———. "Hawks and Moore Battle Leafs Tonight." *Chicago Daily Tribune*, April 7, 1938, 17.

———. "Hawks Beat Americans, 1-0, in 2D Overtime." *Chicago Daily Tribune*, April 1, 1938, 27.

———. "Hawks Meet Canadiens in Series Final." *Chicago Daily Tribune*, March 26, 1938, 21.

———. "Hawks Open Cup Playoff Tonight on Montreal Ice." *Chicago Daily Tribune*, March 22, 1938, 17.

———. "Hawks Seek to Clinch Stanley Cup Tonight." *Chicago Daily Tribune*, April 12, 1938, 27.

———. "Hawks Whip Leafs, 3-1, in First Cup Game." *Chicago Daily Tribune*, April 6, 1938, 23.

———. "Mike Is Back—and the Hawks Mean to Keep Leafs Busy!" *Chicago Daily Tribune*, April 10, 1938, B1.

Stubbs, Dave. "Berlin Blue-Liner Haunted by Morenz's Death." *Gazette* (Montreal, QC), December 31, 2007, 31.

Sullivan, Jack. "Lionel Conacher All-around Athlete in Half-Century of Canadian Sport." *Calgary Herald* (Calgary, AB), December 30, 1950, 22.

"Thomas Henry Coulter." Toronto, ON: Hockey Hall of Fame. https://www.hhof.com/LegendsOfHockey/jsp/SearchPlayer.jsp?player=19861.

Thompson, Paul. "Why Hockey Fans Go Crazy." *Liberty Magazine*, February 17, 1940, 51.

Trautman, Horton. "Hawks, Picked as Sure Losers, Come from Behind to Win." *Chicago Daily News*, date unknown.

———. "Title Unknown." *Chicago Daily News*, April 12, 1938.

Vass, George. *The Chicago Black Hawks Story*. Chicago: Follett Publishing, 1970.

"Virgil Johnson. US Hockey Hall of Fame Defenseman." http://www.virgiljohnson.com.

Wahrman, Ben. "Cully Dahlstrom of Escondido." *San Diego Union*, June 14, 1979, 3.

Ward, Arch. "Fans Spot Each Play Beneath Powerful Light." *Chicago Daily Tribune*, September 1, 1934, 17.

"'We Played Ball According to the Book,' Says Gottselig." *Racine Journal-Times*, September 7, 1943.

Weiskopf, Herm. "An Upsetting Affair. The 1938 Chicago Black Hawks Proved That a Bad Season Means Nothing If You Get a Coach Who Used to Be a Referee." *Sports Illustrated*, March 28, 1960, M8-M12. https://www.si.com/vault/1960/03/28/583839/an-upsetting-affair.

Williams, Dick. "Hell on Skates!" *Liberty Magazine*, February 17, 1934, 36.

"Winter and Summer Sport Stars Meet in Rink Romance at Kansas City." *Edmonton Journal* (Edmonton, AB), March 1, 1935.

Wirth, Louis, and Margaret Furez, eds. *Local Community Fact Book 1938*. Chicago: Chicago Recreation Commission, 1938.

Wong, John. *Lords of the Rinks: The Emergence of the National Hockey League, 1875–1936*. Toronto: University of Toronto Press, 2005.

About the Author

Paul Greenland (www.paulgreenland.com) is the author of *Hockey Chicago Style—The History of the Chicago Blackhawks* (Sagamore Publishing, 1995), an authorized account and one of five comprehensive histories of the team published since 1970. His essay on the Blackhawks appears in *The Encyclopedia of Chicago* (University of Chicago Press, 2004), a project of the Newberry Library in cooperation with the Chicago Historical Society. Greenland is a member of the Society for International Hockey Research and the Chicago Writers Association. He regularly contributes business and career content to reference books from leading publishers. In 2021, Greenland jointly authored *The Vault Guide to Case Interviews, Ninth Edition* (Vault.com Inc.), which *Forbes* calls "CliffsNotes for Careers."